The Essential
Homeschool Kindergarten
Workbook

135 Fun Curriculum-Based Activities to Build Reading, Writing, and Math Skills!

Hayley Lewallen

Illustrations by Collaborate Agency

ROCKRIDGE
PRESS

This book belongs to:

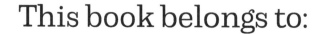

_____

To my boys.

For general information on our other products and services or to obtain technical support, please contact our Customer Care Department within the United States at (866) 744-2665, or outside the United States at (510) 253-0500.

Rockridge Press publishes its books in a variety of electronic and print formats. Some content that appears in print may not be available in electronic books, and vice versa.

TRADEMARKS: Rockridge Press and the Rockridge Press logo are trademarks or registered trademarks of Callisto Media Inc. and/or its affiliates, in the United States and other countries, and may not be used without written permission. All other trademarks are the property of their respective owners. Rockridge Press is not associated with any product or vendor mentioned in this book.

Series Designer: Lisa Schreiber
Interior and Cover Designer: Lisa Schreiber
Art Producer: Samantha Ulban
Editor: Erum Khan
Production Editor: Jenna Dutton
Production Manager: Michael Kay

Illustrations © 2021 Collaborate Agency. Author photo courtesy of Lacey Hinson.

Paperback ISBN: 978-1-63807-021-4

Contents

Part 1: Reading

Print Recognition

Phonics Skills

Part 2: Writing

Part 3: Math

Algebraic Thinking

Measurements and Data

Geometry

Answer Key

Note to Homeschooling Parents

I am so excited that you have chosen this workbook to add to your child's kindergarten experience! This workbook is designed for children ages five to six as a supplemental resource to the kindergarten curriculum. Each activity in this workbook will focus on skills divided into three sections:

Part 1: Reading: These activities build the foundation for learning to read. Letters, sight words, and vocabulary are all key components that will set your child up for success when reading.

Part 2: Writing: This section will help set your child up for success when learning the writing process. Activities include letter writing, vocabulary, simple sentences, sequencing, opinions vs. facts, and more!

Part 3: Math: Numbers, counting, shapes, measurement, addition, subtraction, and more are focused on in these activities.

As an early childhood educator and parent, I have *loved* creating the activities for this workbook! I spent several years teaching kindergarten, and I am truly passionate about this age and set of skills.

A FEW TIPS:

→   Children learn best when they are well rested and eager to learn.
→   You will be reading the directions and any sentences on each page to your child. For the sight word activities, do not encourage your child to sound out the words. These are words that they will need to recognize by sight only.
→   When telling your child the sound that each letter makes, remember that most letters make quick sounds. Try not to add extra vowel sounds at the end of each letter's sound. For example, instead of "tuh" for the letter Tt, the sound should be a quick "t" with air between your teeth.
→   It's important for children to focus on one activity and skill at a time, so they do not feel overwhelmed. Your child can go at their own pace. After all, everyone learns at different speeds. Please allow your child to work at their own pace, which I am sure you are familiar with, while you are homeschooling them. Remember, *you* are your child's biggest cheerleader and support system. If they see you are impressed with their accomplishments in this workbook, that will increase their confidence accordingly.

Now, let's get started!

Exercise Checklist

Below is a checklist to help you keep track of the skills your child has learned and activities they have completed. Check off each activity once finished!

PRINT RECOGNITION

☐ Alphabet Train
☐ Alphabet Train, Continued
☐ Match It Up!
☐ Bug Buddies
☐ Color Match
☐ Pair the Pair
☐ Plane Pals
☐ Letter or Word?
☐ Word or Sentence?
☐ Smiley Spaces

PHONICS SKILLS

☐ What's That Sound?
☐ Match the Letter
☐ This or That
☐ Bubble Letters
☐ Sound Finder
☐ Rhyme Time
☐ Connect the Rhyme
☐ Clap to the Beat
☐ Clap, Count, and Color
☐ Sound Off!
☐ What's the Word?

☐ Middle Match
☐ Vowel Hunt
☐ Which Vowel?
☐ The Perfect Ending
☐ Sounds the Same
☐ Find the Word
☐ Meet the "at" Family
☐ Visit the "ed" Family
☐ The "ig" Family Lives Here
☐ The "op" Family Has Some Fun
☐ Color the "ug" Family
☐ The Long and Short of It
☐ The Great Silent E
☐ Silent E Goes to Work

READING COMPREHENSION

☐ The Playful Pig
☐ A Dog's Bone
☐ Beach Day
☐ The Cat on the Mat
☐ Words You Don't Know
☐ Jim's Rocks
☐ Picture Clues
☐ All about Sharks
☐ A Couple of Caterpillars
☐ Parts of a Book

PRINT SKILLS

☐ ABC Practice
☐ D Is for Dog
☐ G Is for Gorilla
☐ J Is for Jellyfish
☐ M Is for Monkey
☐ P Is for Pig
☐ S Is for Snake
☐ V Is for Volcano
☐ Z Is for Zebra
☐ All the Uppercase Letters
☐ All the Lowercase Letters

LANGUAGE

☐ Flower Power
☐ Sight Word Hide-and-Seek
☐ Crossword Critters
☐ See It and Say It
☐ All-Around Nouns
☐ Draw Your Own
☐ Plural Pictures
☐ Game, Set, Match!
☐ Verbs in Action
☐ What Are They Doing?
☐ Verb and Noun Showdown
☐ All about Firefighters
☐ Question Time!

- ☐ Where, Oh, Where?
- ☐ The Great Outdoors
- ☐ Where Did It Go?
- ☐ A Capital Start
- ☐ Pick the Punctuation
- ☐ Let's Go See the Animals!
- ☐ Match Madness

WRITING SKILLS

- ☐ Your Choice
- ☐ At the Park
- ☐ All about Me
- ☐ Animal Fact Finder
- ☐ That's a Fact
- ☐ The Fact of the Matter
- ☐ How to Brush Your Teeth
- ☐ How to Clean Your Room
- ☐ Think About It
- ☐ Show-and-Tell
- ☐ Jen's Snow Day
- ☐ Pat's Cat
- ☐ Ren Goes to School
- ☐ Mei Plants a Flower

COUNTING

- ☐ Numbers Are Everywhere
- ☐ Number Bugs

- ☐ Fruit Salad
- ☐ Count the Raindrops
- ☐ In the Toy Box
- ☐ Fun in the Sun
- ☐ A Trip to the Candy Shop
- ☐ Summer Reading Challenge
- ☐ Hot Rod Numbers
- ☐ Up to 100!
- ☐ The Case of the Missing Numbers
- ☐ Sunshine Sequence

OPERATIONS IN BASE TEN

- ☐ Count the Blocks
- ☐ Thumbs Up or Down
- ☐ Billy's Blocks
- ☐ Keep on Counting

ALGEBRAIC THINKING

- ☐ Adding Apples
- ☐ Gift Tag Totals
- ☐ Addition Stories
- ☐ Follow the Rainbow
- ☐ Tens Frame Circles
- ☐ Pet Patrol
- ☐ Falling Petals
- ☐ Subtraction Stories
- ☐ School Supplies
- ☐ Fish Friends

MEASUREMENT AND DATA

- ☐ Short and Long
- ☐ Lighten Up
- ☐ Short and Tall
- ☐ More or Less
- ☐ Shipshape
- ☐ Inch by Inch
- ☐ Reach for the Sky

GEOMETRY

- ☐ Flat Shapes
- ☐ Shape Train
- ☐ Do You See It?
- ☐ Corners and Sides
- ☐ The Shape of Things
- ☐ Shape Castle
- ☐ I See in 3D
- ☐ 2D vs. 3D
- ☐ A New Dimension
- ☐ A Lot Alike
- ☐ Shape Builder
- ☐ Hidden Shapes

PART 1
Reading

1. Alphabet Train

Let's review the letters of the alphabet! Here are all 26 letters. When you read the letters, make sure you start on the top row, on the left side—just like when you read a book!

   POINT to each letter and SAY its name out loud. After you say each letter, NAME the picture that starts with that letter. For example: "B, b, ball." Do you hear the "B" at the beginning of "ball"?

➠ Find the very first letter in the alphabet and CIRCLE it! Find the very last letter in the alphabet and UNDERLINE it!

Skill: Alphabet

2. Alphabet Train, Continued

There are five **vowels** in the alphabet: **Aa**, **Ee**, **Ii**, **Oo**, **Uu**. The rest of the letters are **consonants**.

➥ Find all five vowels and CIRCLE them with a red crayon. COUNT the consonants and WRITE down the number in the box.

Skill: Alphabet

3. Match It Up!

Every letter in the alphabet has an **uppercase letter** and a **lowercase letter**.

➡ POINT to and SAY each uppercase letter. FIND and COLOR in the matching lowercase letter. When you've found it, POINT to and SAY each lowercase letter.

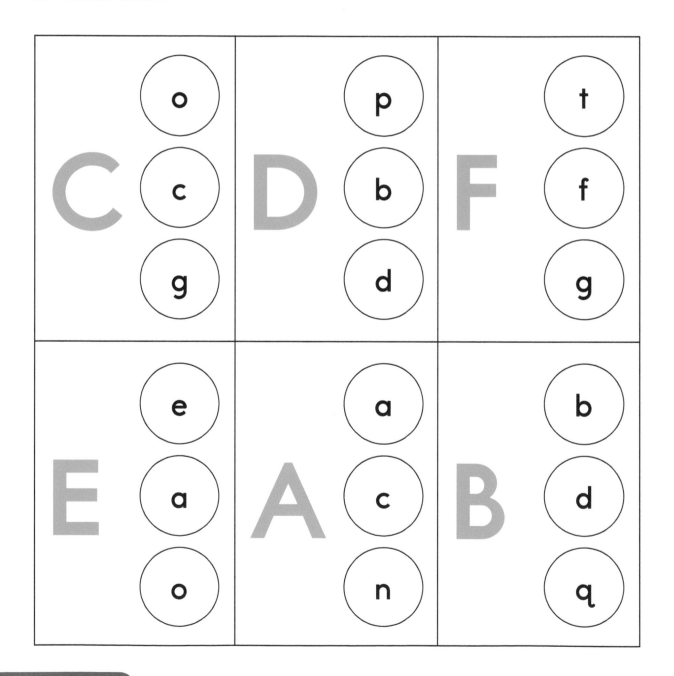

4. Bug Buddies

Every letter in the alphabet has an uppercase letter and a lowercase letter.

➡ POINT to each uppercase letter on the left side and SAY its name. DRAW a line from the uppercase letter to the matching lowercase letter on the right side.

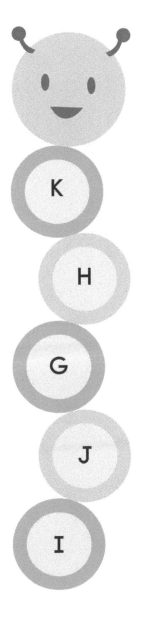
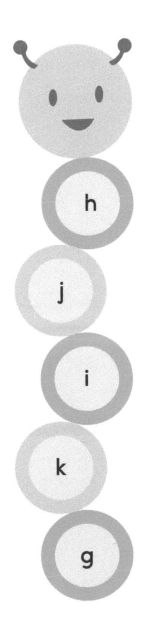

5. Color Match

Every letter in the alphabet has an uppercase letter and a lowercase letter.

➡ COLOR each square using the color in the key that matches the lowercase letter with its uppercase letter.

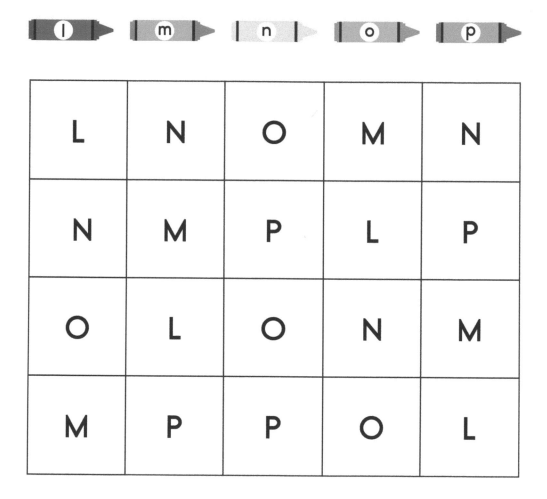

6. Pair the Pair

Every letter in the alphabet has an uppercase letter and a lowercase letter.

➡ POINT to and SAY each uppercase letter. FIND and CIRCLE the matching lowercase letter in the row.

R	a	r	c
Q	q	p	f
T	h	j	t
S	s	r	n
U	a	b	u

Skill: Alphabet

7. Plane Pals

Every letter in the alphabet has an uppercase letter and a
lowercase letter.

➡ POINT to and SAY each letter you see on the airplane. DRAW a line
from each uppercase letter to the matching lowercase letter in the sky.

Skill: Alphabet

8. Letter or Word?

When letters come together, they make **words**! When you see two or more letters together, it is a word. Only **A** and **I** are both letters *and* words!

➡ LOOK at the letters and words below. If it is a letter, CIRCLE it. If it is a word, DRAW a box around it.

Example: (t)   ⬚ dog ⬚

s	hat	t
bed	W	pig
o	p	rag

9. Word or Sentence?

Letters make up words. Words make up **sentences**! A sentence is when words are put together with spaces in between. All sentences start with an uppercase letter and end with punctuation like a **period** (.), **exclamation mark** (!), or a **question mark** (?).

➡ LOOK at each box. If the box has a single word, COLOR it yellow. If the box has a sentence, COLOR it blue.

Example: | the | | I love school! |

| the | The grass is green. | baby |

| I love you! | Do you see it? | see |

| This is fun! | play | I can run. |

| water | I love school! | ball |

10. Smiley Spaces

Sentences are made up of words with spaces between them.
➡ LOOK at each sentence. When you see a space between words, DRAW a smiley face.

I ☺ like ☺ to ☺ play ☺ outside.

I   am   five   years   old.

My   dog   is   black.

Did   you   see   the   book?

Do   you   like   ice   cream?

I   love   jumping!

We   like   to   yell!

11. What's That Sound?

All letters make sounds. When you say a word, the first sound you make tells the letter the word starts with. For example, say the word **book**. Do you hear the "b" sound at the beginning of **book**? This is because the word **book** starts with the letter **B** and **b** says "b."

➡ POINT to each picture and SAY the word. CIRCLE the letter that you hear at the beginning of the word.

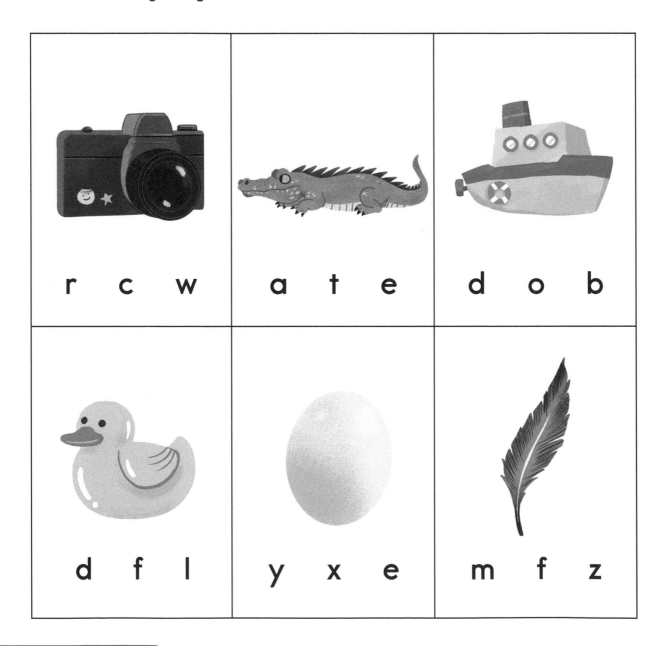

r   c   w   a   t   e   d   o   b

d   f   l   y   x   e   m   f   z

Skill: Letter Sounds

12. Match the Letter

All letters make sounds. When you say a word, the first sound you make tells what letter the word starts with. For example, say the word **horse**. Do you hear the "h" sound at the beginning of **horse**? This is because the word **horse** starts with the letter **H** and **h** says "h."

➡ POINT to each picture and SAY the word. DRAW a line from the picture to the letter you hear at the beginning of the word.

G

H

I

J

K

Skill: Letter Sounds

13. This or That

All letters make sounds. When you say a word, the first sound you make tells us what letter the word starts with. For example, say the word **parrot**. Do you hear the "p" sound at the beginning of **parrot**? This is because the word **parrot** starts with the letter **P** and **p** says "p."

➡ POINT to each picture and SAY the word. CIRCLE the letter you hear at the beginning of the word. DRAW an **X** over the letter you do *not* hear at the beginning of the word.

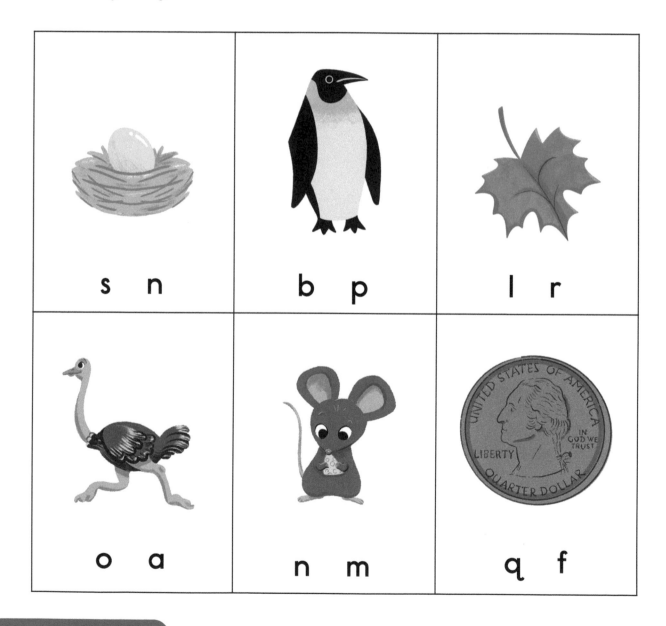

s n	b p	l r
o a	n m	q f

14. Bubble Letters

All letters make sounds. When you say a word, the first sound you make tells what letter the word starts with. For example, say the word **sun**. Do you hear the "s" sound at the beginning of "sun"? This is because the word **sun** starts with the letter **S** and **s** says "s."

➡ POINT to each picture and SAY the word. COLOR in the bubble that shows the letter you hear at the beginning of the word.

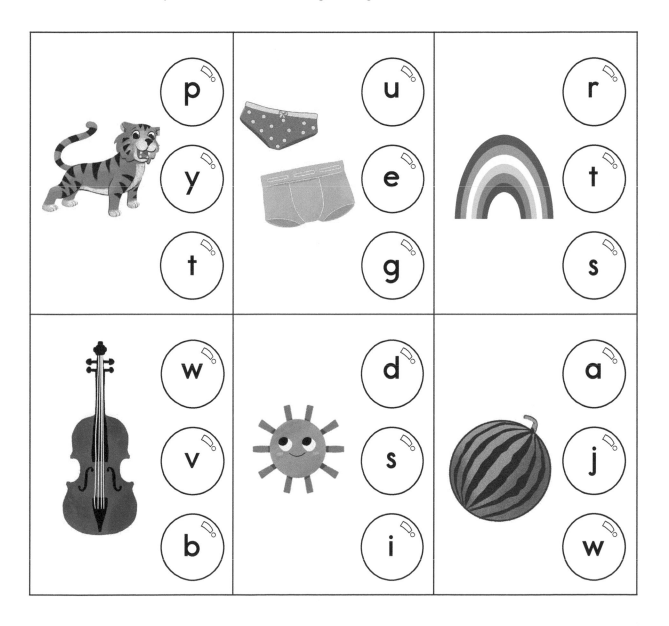

Skill: Letter Sounds

15. Sound Finder

All letters make sounds. When you say a word, the first sound you make tells us what letter the word starts with. For example, say the word **yard**. Do you hear the "y" sound at the beginning of "yarn"? This is because the word **yard** starts with the letter **Y** and **y** says "y."

➡ POINT to each picture and SAY the word. CIRCLE the letter in each row that you hear at the beginning of the word.

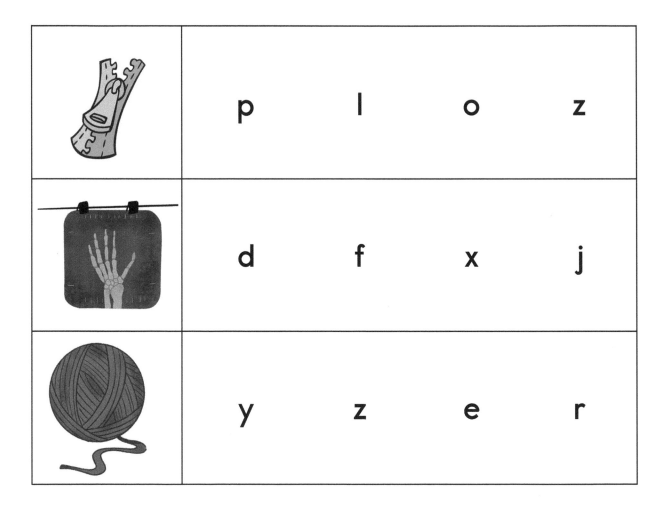

	p	l	o	z
	d	f	x	j
	y	z	e	r

16. Rhyme Time

Rhyming words are words that have the same
ending sound. Words such as **cat** and **hat** rhyme.
Words such as **mouse** and **car** do *not* rhyme.
➡ LOOK at the first picture in each row, and SAY
the word out loud. Then SAY each other word in
the row out loud. LISTEN to hear which word rhymes with the first word.
COLOR the picture of the word that rhymes with the first word, and DRAW
an ✗ over the picture of the word that does not rhyme.

17. Connect the Rhyme

Rhyming words have the same ending sound. Words such as **dog** and **log** rhyme. Words such as **heart** and **ball** do *not* rhyme.

➡ POINT to each picture and SAY the word. DRAW a line between the pictures of the words that rhyme.

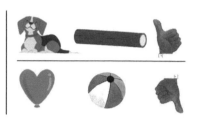

Skill: Rhyming

18. Clap to the Beat

When you say words out loud, each part of a word is called a **syllable**. Syllables always have a vowel in them. An easy way to count syllables is to clap your hands each time you say a part of a word. Let's clap some words together!

These words have only one syllable:

Did you hear how you only clapped one time when you said those words?

These words have two syllables:

Did you hear how you clapped two times when you said those words?

➡ POINT to each picture and SAY the word out loud. CLAP each time you hear a syllable. CIRCLE how many syllables the word has.

baby 1 2	beach ball 1 2	feather 1 2
boat 1 2	kite 1 2	penguin 1 2

Skill: Syllables

19. Clap, Count, and Color

When you say words out loud, each part of a word is called a **syllable**. Syllables always have a vowel in them. An easy way to count syllables is to clap your hands each time you say a part of a word. Let's clap some words together!

These words have two syllables:

Did you hear how you clapped two times when you said those words?

These words have three syllables:

Did you hear how you clapped three times when you said those words?

➡ POINT to each picture, SAY each word, and CLAP for each syllable. How many times did you clap?

➡ COLOR the pictures that have two syllables green. COLOR the pictures that have three syllables purple.

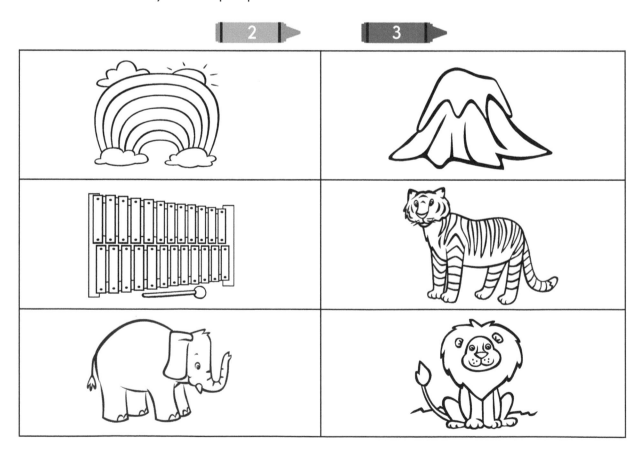

20. Sound Off!

CVC stands for Consonant, Vowel, Consonant. All CVC words have only one syllable. They start with a consonant, have a vowel in the middle (**a, e, i, o, u**), then end with another consonant.

➡ POINT to each picture and SAY the word. LISTEN for the sound you hear at the beginning of the word. CIRCLE the word that matches the picture.

bed | led	run | sun	rat | bat
dad | sad	bug | rug	pig | dig

Skill: Beginning Sounds (CVC Words)

21. What's the Word?

There are always three sounds in CVC words. There is a beginning, middle, and ending sound to make the word.

➡ READ each CVC word. DRAW a line to the matching picture.

net

bug

bag

fox

fan

bus

pot

cup

Skill: Beginning Sounds (CVC Words)

22. Middle Match

CVC words always have a vowel in the middle. Vowels have two sounds: short and long. These are the short vowel sounds:

A says "a" like   E says "e" like   I says "i" like

O says "o" like   U says "u" like

➡ POINT to each picture and SAY the word. LISTEN very carefully to the middle vowel sound you hear when saying the word. CIRCLE the matching word.

hat | hit   sax | six   cut | cat

mud | mad   log | leg   pan | pen

Skill: Beginning Sounds (CVC Words)

23. Vowel Hunt

CVC words always have a vowel in the middle. The vowels are **a**, **e**, **i**, **o**, and **u**.

➡ READ the word in each space. LISTEN closely to what vowel you hear. COLOR each section by matching the word to the color in the key for each vowel sound. What will you reveal after coloring all the spaces?

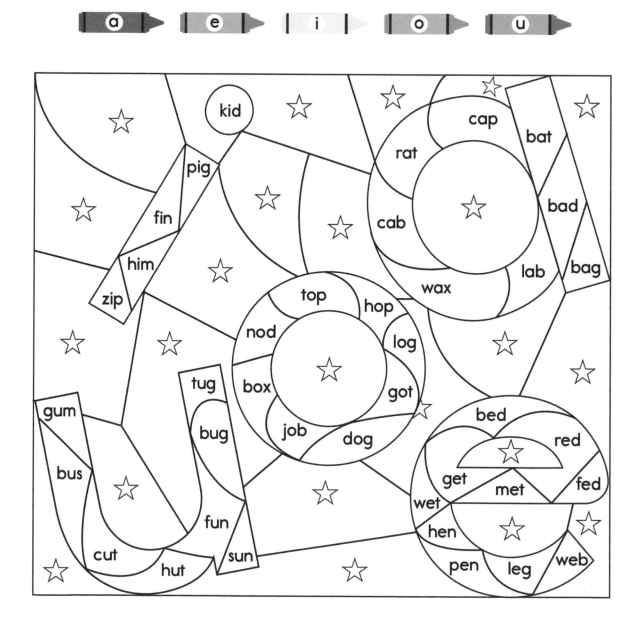

Skill: Short Vowels (CVC Words)

24. Which Vowel?

Vowels always make the middle sound in a CVC word.

➡ POINT to each picture and SAY the word. COLOR the bubble that shows the vowel sound you hear.

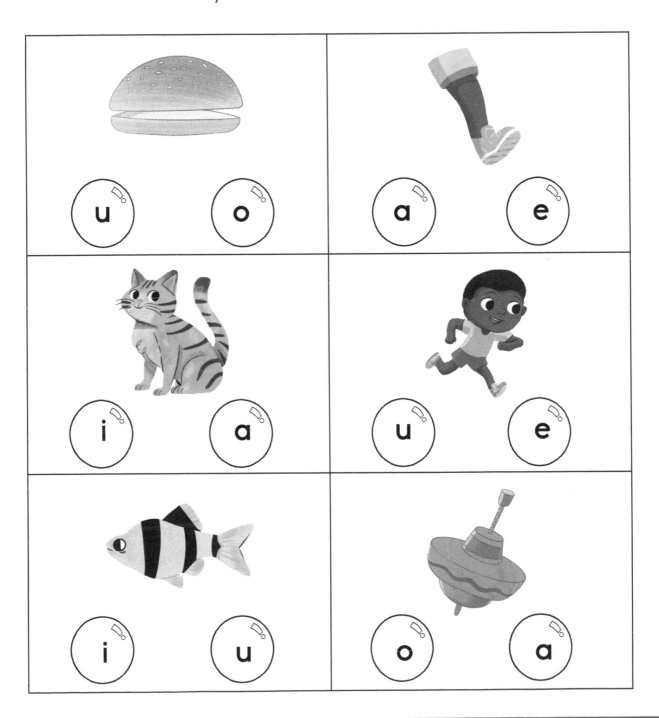

25. The Perfect Ending

CVC words always end with a consonant.

➡ POINT to each picture and say the word. DRAW a line from the picture to the sound you hear at the *end* of the word.

Skill: Ending Sounds (CVC Words)

26. Sounds the Same

CVC words always end with a consonant.

➡ POINT to the first picture in each row and SAY the word. LISTEN carefully to the ending sound. Next, POINT to the other two pictures in the row and SAY the words. COLOR the picture that has the same **ending sound** as the first picture.

Skill: Ending Sounds (CVC Words)

27. Find the Word

Now that you are a master at CVC words, let's see if you can read and match them!

➡ READ a word from the top of the page and FIND the matching picture. WRITE the word below the picture.

fed dad tub jam pin bib

Skill: Reading CVC Words

28. Meet the "at" Family

Word families are groups of words that have the same ending. You can make several different words in a word family by just changing the beginning sound. Let's look at the **at** word family!

➡ Use the letters at the top of the page to FILL IN what's missing in each blank space. Then, READ the word to make sure it matches the picture.

r b h c m

_____ at

_____ at

_____ at

_____ at

_____ at

29. Visit the "ed" Family

Word families are groups of words that have the same ending. You can make several different words in a word family by just changing the beginning sound. Let's look at the **ed** word family!

➡ READ each word. WRITE the word in the boxes, and then CIRCLE the matching picture.

bed	_____	
red	_____	
fed	_____	
wed	_____	
Ted	_____	

Skill: Similar Spellings and Word Families

30. The "ig" Family Lives Here

Word families are groups of words that have the same ending. You can make several different words in a word family by just changing the beginning sound. Let's look at the **ig** word family!

➡ CIRCLE the pictures of words that belong in the **ig** word family. Remember, words that are in the **ig** word family will all have the same "ig" ending sound.

31. The "op" Family Has Some Fun

Word families are groups of words that have the same ending. You can make several different words in a word family by just changing the beginning sound. Let's look at the **op** word family!

➡ READ each sentence. CHOOSE the correct word from the top of the page and WRITE it in the blank.

mop top pop hop

I can spin the _____ .

My brother can _____ the floor.

He can _____ like a bunny.

Don't _____ the balloon!

32. Color the "ug" Family

Word families are groups of words that have the same ending. You can make several different words in a word family by just changing the beginning sound. Let's look at the **ug** word family!

➡ READ each word. COLOR the words that belong in the **ug** word family.

hug	tug	bug	dug
hat	fig	jug	wed
mug	pot	pan	rig
fed	pug	cat	rug

Skill: Similar Spellings and Word Families

33. The Long and Short of It

There are five vowels in the alphabet. **A**, **E**, **I**, **O**, and **U** each make two sounds. They have a short sound and a long sound. These are the vowel sounds:

A says "a" like **apple** or "a" like **acorn**.

E says "e" like **elephant** or "e" like **eagle**.

I says "i" like **igloo** or "i" like **ice cream**.

O says "o" like **octopus** or "o" like **oval**.

U says "u" like **umbrella** or "u" like **unicorn**.

➡ POINT to each letter and SAY its name. POINT to each picture and SAY the word. LISTEN to the beginning sound of each picture. If it starts with either the long or short vowel sound, CIRCLE it. If it does not start with that vowel, DRAW an ✗ on it.

Skill: Long and Short Vowels

34. The Great Silent E

Silent E words are words that have a CVCe pattern. This means they have a Consonant, Vowel, Consonant, and then the letter **e**. The **E** is silent when you say the word, but it magically makes the vowel earlier in the word say its own name (the long sound).

For example, because there is an **e** at the end of the word **rake**, it makes the **a** say its own name when you sound out the word.

rāk<u>e</u>

➼ READ each word and SAY its sound. Remember to make the vowel say its own name because of the silent E.

➼ READ each word. DRAW a line to the matching picture.

kite

robe

cane

tape

cape

35. Silent E Goes to Work

A **silent E** works by making a vowel say its own name. Try sounding out this **silent E** word:

cūb<u>e</u>

➡ READ each sentence. CHOOSE the correct word from the top of the page and WRITE it in the blank.

| bone   bike   time   hive   home |

The dog has a _____.

A clock tells us the _____.

I like to ride my_____.

My family lives in a _____.

Bees make honey in a _____.

36. The Playful Pig

There are always **key details** in stories. Key details are the important parts of stories like **who**, **what**, **when**, **where**, or **why**.

➡ READ the short story. LISTEN carefully for the key details. READ the questions and CIRCLE the correct answer.

Pig likes the mud. He plays in the mud at the farm. He gets very dirty. He needs a bath.

Who likes to play in the mud?

pig   dog

Where does he play in the mud?

in the house   at the farm

What does he need after playing in the mud?

a bath   a cookie

Skill: Key Details

37. A Dog's Bone

There are always **key details** in stories. Key details are the important parts of stories like **who, what, when, where,** or **why.**

➡ READ the short story. LISTEN carefully for the key details. READ the questions and use the words from the top of the page to WRITE in the correct answer.

bone Spot backyard

I have a dog named Spot. I gave Spot a bone. He buried it in the backyard. He loves to bury his bones.

What is the dog's name?

_____

What did the child give the dog?

_____

Where did the dog bury it?

_____

Skill: Key Details

38. Beach Day

Connecting ideas from stories will help you remember and understand them better. When you connect a story to yourself, you might think about how you might have had a similar experience to what happened in the story.
➥ READ the story. THINK about a time in your life that reminds you about this story. It may be a time you went to the beach, or just a trip you went on. DRAW a picture and WRITE a sentence to match.

When I was little, I went to the beach. I helped my mom pack my suitcase. We drove in the car for a long time to get to the beach. My favorite part about the beach was playing in the sand. I was sad when we had to come home.

Skill: Connecting Ideas

39. The Cat on the Mat

A **sequence** is the order in which something happens. Words such as **first**, **next**, **then**, and **last** describe a sequence. You could also use numbers to sequence something. When reading stories, it is important to remember the sequence of things happening.

➡ READ the story. LISTEN carefully to the sequence of events. WRITE a **1** in the box of the picture that happened first, a **2** in the second event, and a **3** in the third event.

The cat is cute and orange. The cat ate his lunch. The cat took a nap on the blue mat.

Skill: Connecting Ideas

40. Words You Don't Know

Unknown words are words that you might not know how to read yet, or words that you don't know the meaning of. When reading a book, you can use the pictures as clues to help figure out an unknown word.
➡ READ each sentence. LOOK at the picture. Use a word from the top of the page to WRITE in the word that makes sense.

> leaves water bird
> sandcastles shoulders

My dad puts me on his _____.

We like to build _____ at the beach.

Flowers need sunlight, soil, and _____ to live.

Penguins are a type of _____.

I use a rake to gather _____.

41. Jim's Rocks

Unknown words are words that you might not know how to read yet, or words that you don't know the meaning of. When reading a book, you can use the other words in the sentence to figure out an unknown word.
➡ READ the story. Pay attention to the words that are underlined and think about what they mean. READ the questions below and CIRCLE the correct word meaning.

Jim loves to <u>collect</u> rocks. His favorite place to <u>discover</u> rocks is by the creek. Jim has 43 rocks with different <u>lusters</u>. What is something you like to collect?

What do you think the word <u>collect</u> means?

☐ gather ☐ eat

What do you think the word <u>discover</u> means?

☐ cook ☐ find

What do you think the word <u>lusters</u> means?

☐ shininess ☐ faces

Skill: Unknown Words

42. Picture Clues

You can use the clues you find in pictures to predict what a story might be about.

➥ These pictures are all from a book. LOOK at each picture. CIRCLE what you think the book might be about.

	☐ a sleepy cat ☐ a hungry monkey
	☐ a train ride ☐ a rainy day
	☐ a slumber party ☐ a day at the zoo
	☐ a baseball game ☐ a day at school

Skill: Picture Clues

43. All about Sharks

An author is a person who writes a story or informational text. When an author writes informational text, they are trying to teach us something that is true. These are called **facts**.

➡ READ the story. UNDERLINE each sentence that tells a fact.

Sharks live in the ocean. Sharks have many teeth that they lose and replace often. Sharks cannot see color. Most sharks live for about 25 years. Have you ever seen a shark?

Skill: Text Support

44. A Couple of Caterpillars

Sometimes books can have the same topic but tell a different story. You can compare how the books are the same and how they are different.
➡ READ each story. READ the questions below and CIRCLE the correct answer. FILL IN the answer for the last question.

CAM LOVES BOOKS

Cam the caterpillar loves to read books. His favorite book is about a teddy bear. Cam also likes to play basketball and go fishing.

CASSIE LOVES DOLLS

Cassie the caterpillar loves to play with her dolls. Her favorite doll has a blue dress and red hair. Cassie also likes to go fishing and wants to be a scientist when she grows up.

What are both of these stories about?

☐ caterpillars   ☐ monkeys

What is one thing that they both like to do?

☐ basketball   ☐ fishing

How are Cam and Cassie different?

_____

Skill: Compare and Contrast Texts

45. Parts of a Book

Books have many different parts. They have a **front cover**, a **back cover**, and a **spine** to hold in all the pages.

➡ Use the words at the top of the page to label the parts of a book.

front cover	back cover	spine

Skill: Book Structure

PART 2
Writing

1. ABC Practice

It's time to practice writing your letters!
➡ TRACE each letter by following the arrows. Then practice writing the letters by yourself on the lines.

2. D Is for Dog

It's time to keep practicing writing your letters!

➡ TRACE each letter by following the arrows. Then practice writing the letter on the lines.

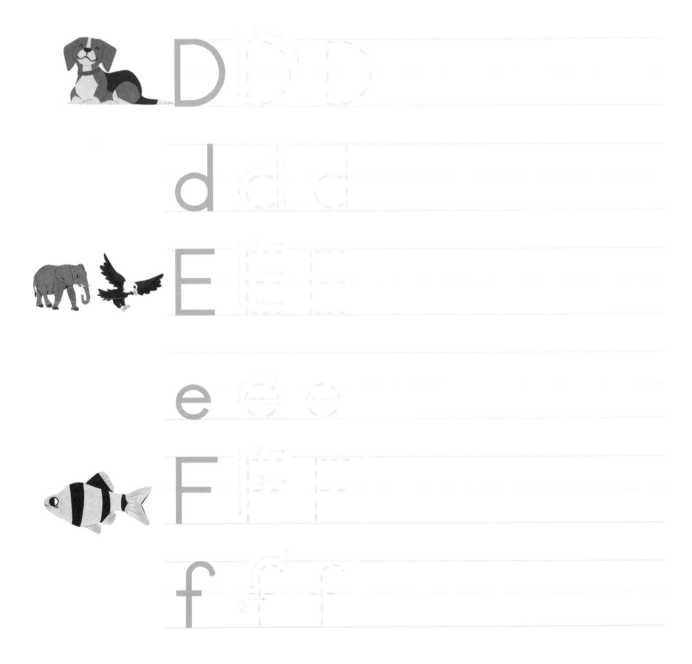

Skill: Writing Letters

3. G Is for Gorilla

It's time to keep practicing writing your letters!
➡ TRACE each letter by following the arrows. Then practice writing the letter on the lines.

4. J Is for Jellyfish

It's time to keep practicing writing your letters!

➡ TRACE each letter by following the arrows. Then practice writing the letter on the lines.

5. M Is for Monkey

It's time to keep practicing writing your letters!

➡ TRACE each letter by following the arrows. Then practice writing the letter on the lines.

6. P Is for Pig

It's time to keep practicing writing your letters!

➡ TRACE each letter by following the arrows. Then practice writing the letter on the lines.

7. S Is for Snake

It's time to keep practicing writing your letters!
➡ TRACE each letter by following the arrows. Then practice writing the letter on the lines.

8. V Is for Volcano

It's time to keep practicing writing your letters!

➡ TRACE each letter by following the arrows. Then practice writing the letter on the lines.

Skill: Writing Letters

9. Z Is for Zebra

➥ TRACE each letter by following the arrows. Then practice writing the letter on the lines.

10. All the Uppercase Letters

Now that you have practiced writing all of the uppercase letters in the alphabet, you can write them in alphabetical order!

➡ Start with tracing **A**. Then FILL IN the missing letters all the way to **Z**.

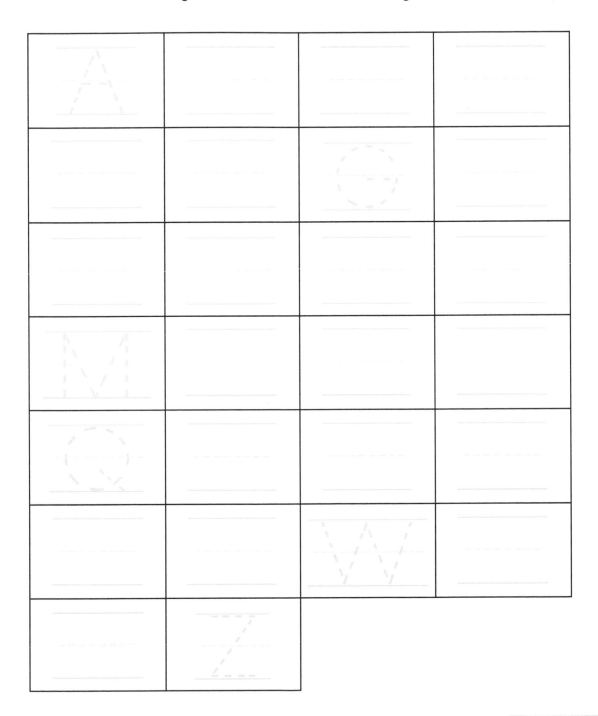

11. All the Lowercase Letters

Now that you have practiced writing all of the lowercase letters in the alphabet, you can write them in alphabetical order!

➥ Start with tracing **a**. Then FILL IN the missing letters all the way to **z**.

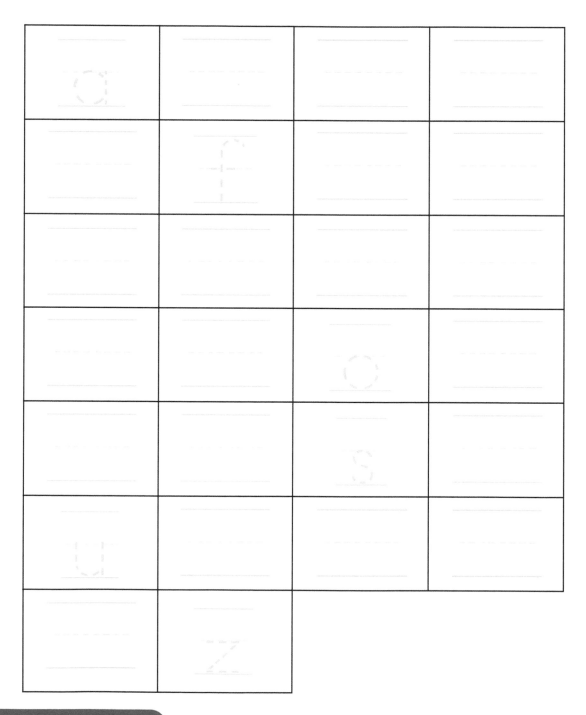

Skill: Writing Letters

12. Flower Power

Sight words are words that should be recognized quickly just by looking at them instead of sounding them out.

➻ *Parents: READ each word to your child if they do not recognize it.*

➻ POINT to each word and SAY it out loud.

the of you she my

➻ READ each word on the flowers. COLOR each flower using the color in the key that matches the word.

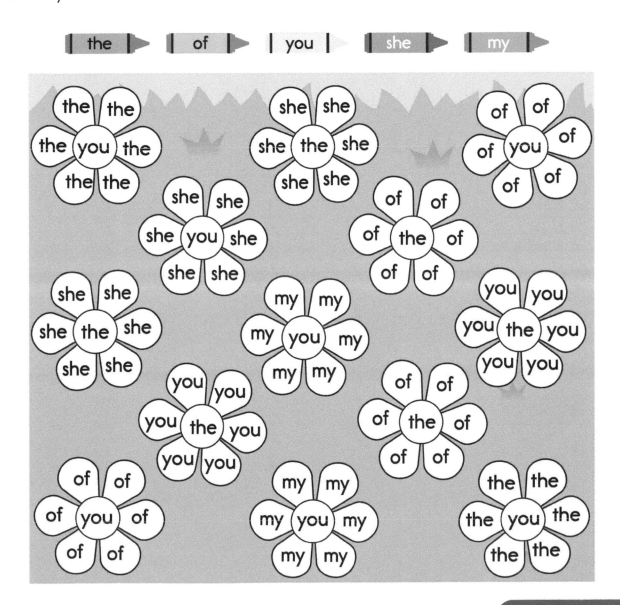

| the ▶ | of ▶ | you | she ▶ | my ▶ |

13. Sight Word Hide-and-Seek

Sight words are words that should be recognized quickly just by looking at them, instead of sounding them out.

➡ *Parents: READ each word to your child if they do not recognize it.*

➡ POINT to each word, and SAY it out loud.

is are do we see

➡ Oh no! The words are all hidden! LOOK carefully for each sight word listed above. CIRCLE all five sight words.

s	a	r	e	r	f
a	b	h	n	j	g
l	s	s	i	i	s
o	c	e	d	a	y
s	w	e	w	z	p
k	u	l	x	d	o
r	t	v	m	n	q

Skill: Sight Words

14. Crossword Critters

Sight words are words that should be recognized quickly just by looking at them, instead of sounding them out.

➠ *Parents: READ each word to your child if they do not recognize it.*

➠ POINT to each word and SAY it out loud.

at went they what saw

➠ FILL IN the blanks of the crossword puzzle using the five sight words listed above.

15. See It and Say It

Sight words are words that should be recognized quickly just by looking at them, instead of sounding them out.

➠ *Parents: READ each word to your child if they do not recognize it.*

➠ POINT to each word and SAY it out loud.

eat get good like with

➠ READ each sentence and LOOK at the picture. CHOOSE the correct sight word from above and WRITE it in the blank space.

1. I love to _____ apples.

2. I will _____ a book off the shelf.

3. We like pizza _____ pepperoni on top.

4. This cookie is _____.

5. I look _____ my dad.

16. All-Around Nouns

Nouns are everywhere. They are words that name a person, place, or thing.

PERSON   PLACE   THING

➡ Is it a person, place, or thing? COLOR the pictures below by matching the color to the key above.

17. Draw Your Own

Nouns are everywhere. They are words that name a person, place, or thing.
➡ LOOK at each image for an example of a person, place, or thing. DRAW your own person, place, and thing in the boxes.

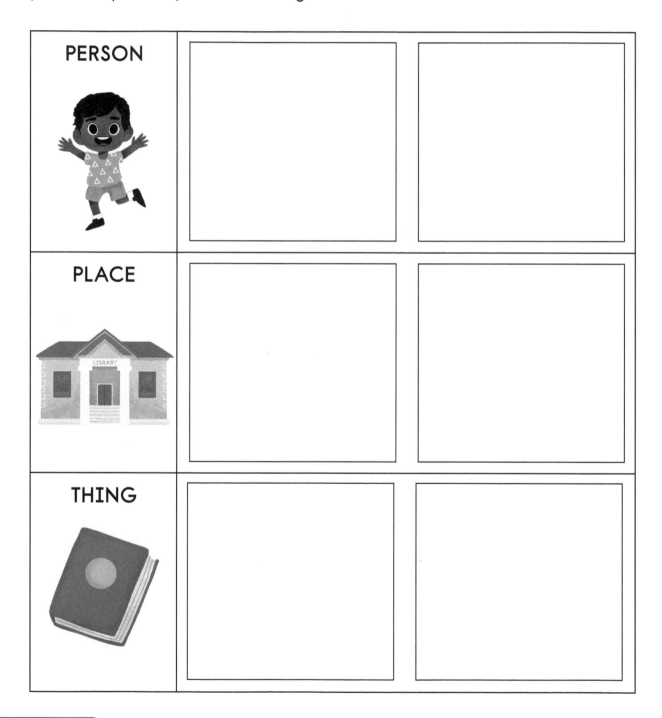

18. Plural Pictures

Singular means there is only one thing. **Plural** means that there is *more* than one thing. The plural form of a word adds an "s" or "es" sound to the end of the word.

For example, if you want to say the plural of the word **cat**, you say **cats**. That means there is more than one cat.

cat ➡ cats

➥ LOOK at each picture. READ the two word choices. CIRCLE the correct word.

➥ *Parents: The focus of this activity is to listen to the ending sound to hear if the word is singular or plural. If your child cannot read these words yet, please read for them and let the child listen to each ending.*

dog | dogs   car | cars   tree | trees

bus | buses   heart | hearts   dress | dresses

Skill: Nouns

19. Game, Set, Match!

Singular means there is only one thing. **Plural** means that there is more than one thing. The plural form of a word adds an "s" or "es" sound to the end of the word.

For example, if you want to say the plural of the word **pencil**, you say **pencils**. That means there is more than one pencil.

pencil ➜ pencils

➥ READ each word. DRAW a line from the word to the matching box that shows the picture or set of pictures.

➥ *Parents: The focus of this activity is to listen to the ending sound to hear if the word is singular or plural. If your child cannot read these words yet, please read for them and let the child listen to each ending.*

brushes

box

pig

brush

pigs

boxes

Skill: Nouns

20. Verbs in Action

Verbs are action words. When you hear a verb in a sentence, it means an action is happening. Words such as **running** and **walking** are verbs.

➡ CIRCLE the pictures that show a verb.

playing	pig	flying
baby	looking	swimming
reading	house	shirt

Skill: Verbs

21. What Are They Doing?

Verbs are action words. When you hear a verb in a sentence, it means an action is happening. Words such as **play** and **throw** are verbs.

➡ READ each verb. DRAW a line to match the word to the correct picture.

write

drive

talk

cook

watch

Skill: Verbs

22. Verb and Noun Showdown

Nouns are words that name a person, place, or thing. **Verbs** are action words. When you hear a verb in a sentence, it means an action is happening.

➡ LOOK at each picture. CHOOSE a word from the top of the page to describe each picture and WRITE it in the blank space. CIRCLE whether it is a noun or verb.

eat dog sleep rabbit swim cry

_____ noun | verb	_____ noun | verb	_____ noun | verb
_____ noun | verb	_____ noun | verb	_____ noun | verb

Skill: Nouns vs. Verbs

23. All about Firefighters

When reading and writing, it is important to understand **question words**. These are questions like **who**, **what**, **when**, **where**, **why**, and **how**.
➡ READ each question and CIRCLE the best answer.

Who helps put out fires?	
What tool does a firefighter use?	
Where do firefighters work when they are not putting out fires?	
How do firefighters get to the fires?	

Skill: Question Words

24. Question Time!

When reading and writing, it is important to understand **question words**. These are questions like **who**, **what**, **when**, **where**, **why**, and **how**.
➡ READ each sentence. FILL IN the blanks with the word from the top of the page that fits the best in each sentence.

| Who What When Where Why How |

1. _____ should we go to see the animals?

2. _____ did this nest get in the tree?

3. _____ helps us feel better?

4. _____ food do I need to buy from the store?

5. _____ will we have your graduation party?

6. _____ do squirrels gather nuts?

25. Where, Oh, Where?

Prepositions are also called **positional words**. These are words that tell *where* something is. Look at each picture of the boy and the box to see *where* he is.

➡ LOOK at each picture. CIRCLE the correct preposition that describes where the smaller object is.

BEHIND | BELOW

IN | ON

BELOW | BETWEEN

BETWEEN | BEHIND

IN | ON

BEHIND | BY

Skill: Prepositions

26. The Great Outdoors

Prepositions are also known as **positional words**. These are words that tell *where* something is. Look at each picture of the boy and the box to see *where* he is.

➡ READ each sentence. FOLLOW the directions.

Draw an apple <u>on</u> the tree.

Draw the sun <u>between</u> the clouds.

Circle the boy <u>behind</u> the tree.

Draw a bird <u>below</u> a cloud.

Draw a picture of yourself <u>by</u> the flower.

Skill: Prepositions

27. Where Did It Go?

Prepositions are also known as **positional words**. These are words that tell *where* something is.

on in by behind below between

➡ READ each sentence. LOOK at the picture and CHOOSE the correct word from the top of the page to FILL IN the blank space.

The bear is _____ the wagon.	The boy is _____ the kite.
The girl is _____ the chair.	The monkey is _____ the trees.
The table is _____ the couch.	The cat is _____ the rug.

Skill: Prepositions

28. A Capital Start

The very first letter in every sentence must start with an uppercase, or **capital**, letter. Take a look at what capital letters look like. Can you point to each letter and say its name?

A B C D E F G H I J K L M N O P Q R S T U V W X Y Z

➡ Each sentence is missing a **capital letter** at the beginning. WRITE each sentence again on the line and make the first letter a capital.

birds can fly.

_____

koalas can climb.

_____

monkeys like bananas.

_____

fish have gills.

_____

birds eat bugs.

_____

Skill: Capitalization

29. Pick the Punctuation

Sentences always end with **punctuation marks**. There are three types of punctuation marks that can go at the end of a sentence.

Types of punctuation:

• PERIOD

These sentences *tell* us something.

I ride the bus to school.

! EXCLAMATION MARK

These sentences are when we *shout* something.

I am so excited!

? QUESTION MARK

These sentences are when we *ask* a question.

Do you like cheese?

➡ READ each sentence. COLOR in the box with the correct punctuation.

No way	☐ .	☐ !	☐ ?
My bike is green	☐ .	☐ !	☐ ?
What is your name	☐ .	☐ !	☐ ?
Her ball is big	☐ .	☐ !	☐ ?
Look at me	☐ .	☐ !	☐ ?
How old are you	☐ .	☐ !	☐ ?

Skill: Punctuation

30. Let's Go See the Animals!

Complete sentences start with a capital letter and end with a punctuation mark.

➡ LOOK at each sentence. CIRCLE each capital letter at the beginning of the sentence in green. CIRCLE the punctuation at the end of the sentence in red.

The monkey likes bananas.

An octopus has eight legs.

That elephant is huge!

Pigs like to roll in mud.

How do fish move?

There's a snake!

What do rabbits eat?

Skill: Complete Sentences

31. Match Madness

Complete sentences start with a capital letter and end with a punctuation mark.

➡ READ each complete sentence. DRAW a line from the sentence to its matching picture.

I see a big bed.

I like to dig.

I see a fan.

The dog can sit.

The cat is orange.

My rug is red.

Skill: Complete Sentences

32. Your Choice

Opinions are the way people feel about things. Everyone can have different opinions. You might think summer is better than winter, but your friend might like winter more. It is okay to have different opinions!

➡ COMPARE each set of choices. CIRCLE the option that you like better.

apples		OR	bananas	
cookie		OR	cupcake	
sun		OR	snow	
cats		OR	dogs	
bike		OR	scooter	

Skill: Opinions

33. At the Park

Opinions are the way people feel about things. Everyone can have different opinions. You might think dogs are better than cats, but your friend might like cats more. It is okay to have different opinions!

When you have an opinion on something, you always have a reason. You might like dogs more than cats because you like walking your dog on a leash. Your friend might like cats more because they purr.

➡ CIRCLE which activity at the park you think is better. Then WRITE which activity you like and give a reason you like it.

SLIDE OR SWING?

I like to _____

because _____

_____

_____

_____

_____

_____.

34. All about Me

Facts are when you write about things that have been proven true.

    For example, a fact about dogs is that they have puppies.

➡ DRAW a picture of yourself and WRITE three facts all about *you!*

35. Animal Fact Finder

Informational writing is when you write about real things. Informational writing contains **facts**. These are statements with information that has been proven true.

For example, a fact about spiders is that they have eight legs.

➡ What is your favorite animal? DRAW a picture of that animal and WRITE as many facts about it as you can.

My Animal: _____

_____

_____

_____

_____

_____

Skill: Facts

36. That's a Fact

A **fact** is information that has been proven true. **Opinions** are how someone feels about something. Here is an example:

JELLYFISH
Fact: Jellyfish can sting you.
Opinion: I do not like jellyfish!

➡ READ each sentence. CIRCLE whether it is a fact or opinion.

Fish have scales.		FACT | OPINION
Insects are cool.		FACT | OPINION
A lion's baby is a cub.		FACT | OPINION
An eagle is a type of bird.		FACT | OPINION
Baby elephants are so cute.		FACT | OPINION
A rabbit is a fun pet.		FACT | OPINION

Skill: Fact and Opinion

37. The Fact of the Matter

A **fact** is information that has been proved true. **Opinions** are how someone feels about something.

➡ LOOK at the picture. Then READ each sentence. COLOR the sentence box yellow if it is an opinion. Color the sentence box green if it is a fact.

Here is an example:

| ICE CREAM | Ice cream is cold. |
| | Ice cream is the best dessert. |

TURTLE	Turtles have shells.
	Turtles are cool animals.
IGLOO	I would love to live in an igloo.
	Igloos are made of ice.
HORSE	Horses can gallop.
	I like to ride horses.
BOAT	Boats are fun to watch.
	Boats can float on water.
FROG	Frogs lay eggs.
	Frogs are neat.

Skill: Fact and Opinion

38. How to Brush Your Teeth

Informational writing is when you write about real things. You could write about yourself, animals, tractors, how to do something, or anything that you know a lot about!

We brush our teeth every day. THINK about the steps you take to brush your teeth. DRAW a picture and/or WRITE a sentence in each box to show each step.

HOW TO BRUSH YOUR TEETH

> **FIRST**

> **THEN**

> **FINALLY**

Skill: Informational Texts

39. How to Clean Your Room

Informational writing is when you write about real things. You could write about anything that you know a lot about!

➡ Cleaning up is very important. THINK about the steps you take to clean your room. DRAW a picture and/or WRITE a sentence in each box to show each step.

HOW TO CLEAN YOUR ROOM

FIRST

THEN

FINALLY

Skill: Informational Texts

40. Think About It

Informational writing is when you write about real things. Sometimes, authors use graphic organizers to write out their facts before writing their sentences.

➡ THINK about something you know a lot about. WRITE the topic on the line. THINK of facts about it, and WRITE the facts in the thought bubbles.

TOPIC: _____

Skill: Informational Texts

41. Show-and-Tell

Informational writing is when you write about real things. You could write about anything that you know a lot about!

➡ CHOOSE a topic that you know a lot about.

DRAW a picture and WRITE at least two facts about it.

_____

_____

_____

_____

Skill: Informational Texts

42. Jen's Snow Day

Sequencing is the order in which things happened. When listening to stories, it is important to pay attention to what happens in the beginning, middle, and end of the story.

➡ READ the short story. DRAW pictures in the boxes of what happened at the **beginning**, **middle**, and **end** of the story.

Jen woke up and wanted to play in the snow. She got dressed and put on all of her warm winter clothes. She went outside and played in the snow!

BEGINNING	MIDDLE	END

Skill: Story Sequencing

43. Pat's Cat

Sequencing is the order in which things happened. When listening to stories, it is important to pay attention to what happens **first**, **second**, **third**, and on and on.

➡ Pat got a new cat! LOOK at each picture to see what happened **first**, **second**, and **third**. READ each sentence and FILL IN the blank.

First, Pat got a new _____.

Next, Pat gave his cat _____.

Last, Pat played with his cat with a _____.

Skill: Story Sequencing

44. Ren Goes to School

Sequencing is the order in which things happened. When listening to stories or seeing pictures, it is important to understand what happens **first**, **second**, **third**, **fourth**, and on and on.

➡ READ the title and LOOK at each picture. Use the numbers **1**, **2**, **3**, and **4** to put the pictures in order.

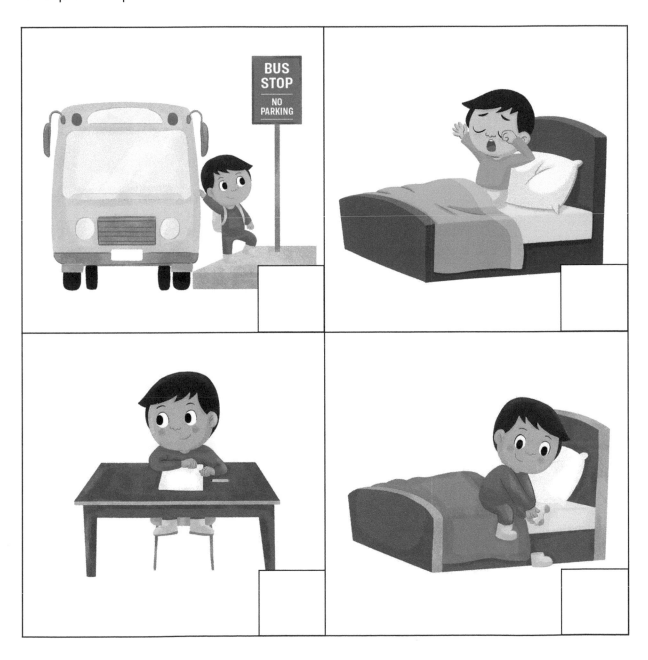

Skill: Story Sequencing

45. Mei Plants a Flower

Sequencing is the order in which things happened. When hearing stories or seeing pictures, it is important to understand what happens **first**, **second**, **third**, **fourth**, and on and on.

➡ READ the title and LOOK at each picture. Use the numbers **1**, **2**, **3**, and **4** to put the pictures in order.

Skill: Story Sequencing

PART 3

Math

1. Numbers Are Everywhere

Numbers are everywhere. Numbers tell *how many* there are of something.

➡ POINT to each number and SAY its name. COUNT the objects next to each number. CIRCLE the number **0**. UNDERLINE the number **20**.

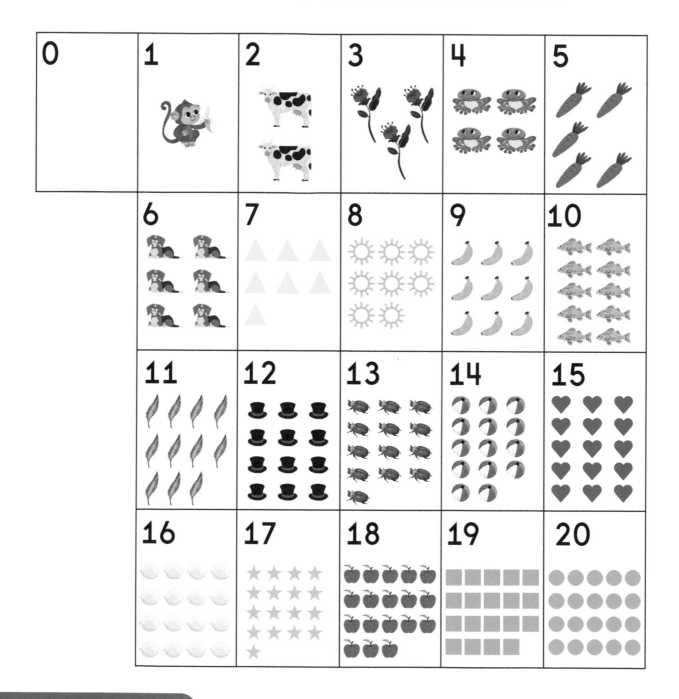

2. Number Bugs

Numbers **0** to **9** are numbers that you will see in every other number. For example, the number **10** is made up of the numbers **1** and **0**.

➡ TRACE the numbers. FILL IN the missing numbers.

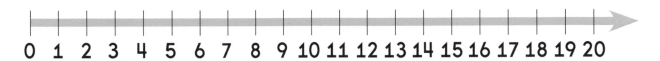

0 1 2 3 4 5 6 7 8 9 10 11 12 13 14 15 16 17 18 19 20

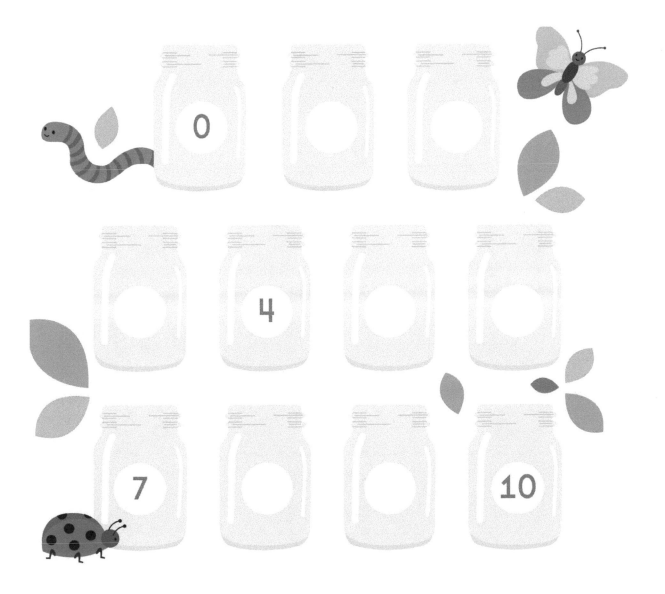

3. Fruit Salad

It is important to count things one at a time. You can use your finger to point to and touch each object as you count it.

➡ COUNT each set of fruit. To help keep track of which fruit you have counted, you can cross it out as you count. CIRCLE the correct number.

0 1 2 3 4 5 6 7 8 9 10 11 12 13 14 15 16 17 18 19 20

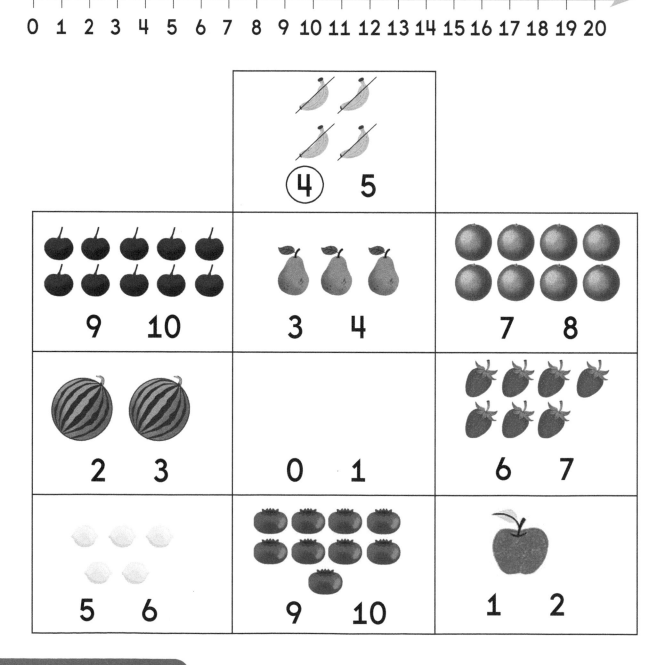

Skill: Counting 0 to 10

4. Count the Raindrops

After the number **10** comes the number **11**. The numbers from **11** to **19** are also known as "teen" numbers.

➡ TRACE the numbers. FILL IN the missing numbers.

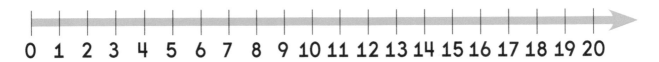

0 1 2 3 4 5 6 7 8 9 10 11 12 13 14 15 16 17 18 19 20

5. In the Toy Box

It is important to count objects one at a time. You can use your finger to point to and touch each object as you count it.

➡ LOOK at each number. COLOR IN that number of toys.

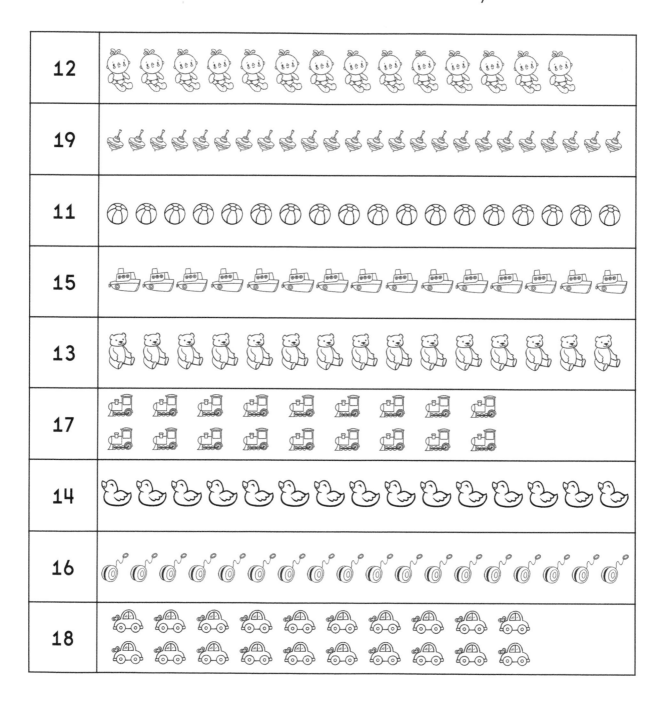

Skill: Counting 11 to 20

6. Fun in the Sun

It is important to count things one at a time. You can use your finger to point to and touch each object as you count it.

➡ COUNT each set of objects. WRITE the correct number in the blank space.

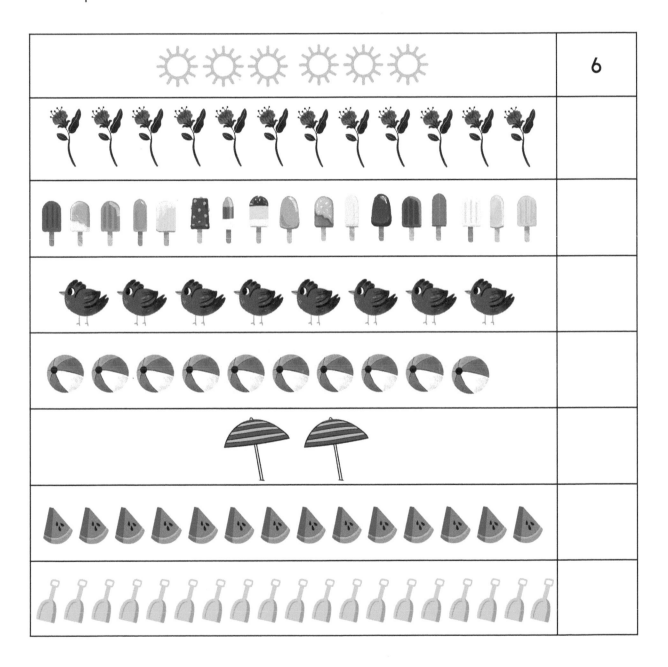

☼ ☼ ☼ ☼ ☼ ☼	6
flowers	
popsicles	
birds	
beach balls	
umbrellas	
watermelon slices	
shovels	

7. A Trip to the Candy Shop

Counting tells *how many* there are of something. When you add one more to a group, the total is the next number up.

For example, pretend you have five pieces of candy in your hand. You get one more piece. How many do you have now? Six!

➡ COUNT each set of objects. Add one more in your head. Use the number line if you need help. DRAW a line from the objects to the number that show one more than the set.

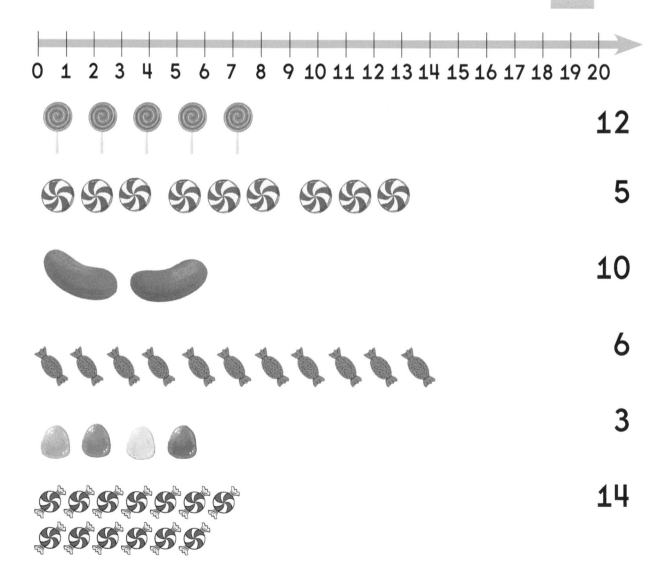

Skill: One More

8. Summer Reading Challenge

Graphs give us information and can help us compare numbers.

When comparing numbers, we use words and phrases like **more**, **less**, **greater than**, **less than**, **fewer**, or **equal to**. For example, when comparing two numbers that are the same, they are **equal to** each other.

➡ The kids finished a reading challenge last summer. This graph shows how many books they each read. COUNT how many books each child read and WRITE the number. WRITE the answers to the below questions.

 = 1 book

Nate	📘📘📘	
Aisha	📘📘📘📘	
Jamal	📘📘📘📘📘📘	
Wendy	📘📘📘📘	
Kevin	📘📘📘📘📘📘📘📘	

Who read the most books?

_____

Who read the least books?

_____

Who read more books than Jamal? _____

Who read fewer books than Aisha?

_____

Which two kids read an equal number of books?

_____

Skill: Comparing Numbers

9. Hot Rod Numbers

When comparing numbers, we use words and phrases like **more**, **less**, **greater than**, **less than**, **fewer**, or **equal to**.

➡ COUNT each set of cars. COMPARE the sets. COLOR the boxes by matching the answer to the colors in the key.

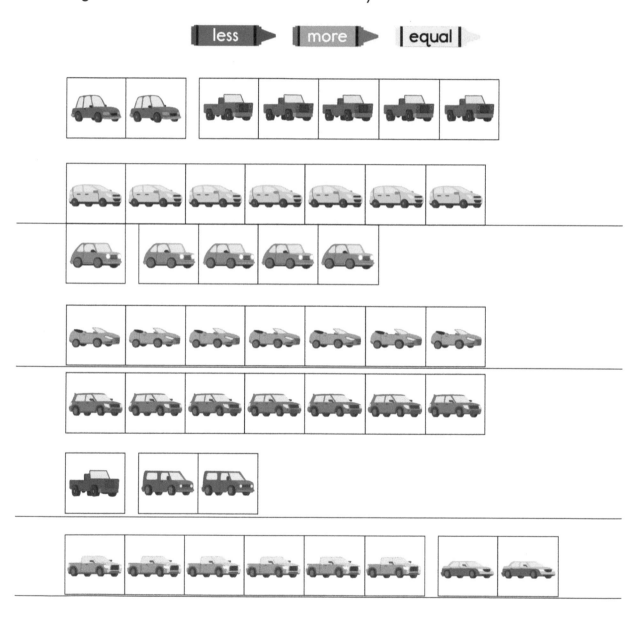

10. Up to 100!

A **hundreds** chart is when you see the numbers **1** to **100** written out in rows of **10**. When counting by **ones**, you say each number on the **hundreds** chart. When counting by **tens**, you say only the numbers that end in **0**.

➡ Practice counting to **100** by **ones**. POINT to each number and SAY it out loud.

➡ Practice counting to **100** by **tens**. Start with the number **10** and POINT to each number that ends with **0**. After you have counted, COLOR the boxes yellow that you counted by **tens**.

1	2	3	4	5	6	7	8	9	10
11	12	13	14	15	16	17	18	19	20
21	22	23	24	25	26	27	28	29	30
31	32	33	34	35	36	37	38	39	40
41	42	43	44	45	46	47	48	49	50
51	52	53	54	55	56	57	58	59	60
61	62	63	64	65	66	67	68	69	70
71	72	73	74	75	76	77	78	79	80
81	82	83	84	85	86	87	88	89	90
91	92	93	94	95	96	97	98	99	100

Skill: Numbers 1 to 100

11. The Case of the Missing Numbers

A **hundreds** chart is when you see the numbers **1** to **100** written out in rows of **10**. When we count by **ones**, we say each number on the **hundreds** chart. When we count by **tens**, you say only the numbers that end in **0**.

➡ TRACE the numbers you see and FILL IN the missing numbers from **1** to **100**.

1		3	4		6		8		10
11		13		15	16		18		
21			24			27	28	29	
	32	33		35		37			40
	42				46			49	
51		53		55		57	58	59	60
	63		65	66		68			
71	72		74		76			79	80
81		83		85		87	88		
	92	93		95			98		100

Skill: Numbers 1 to 100

12. Sunshine Sequence

Counting on is when you start at a given number and count up.

➥ READ each number. FILL IN the numbers that come next and continue the sequence for each row.

12

45

3

86

22

13. Count the Blocks

Each place in a number is given a value that can be shown with **base ten blocks**. One base ten block represents **1**. You count these by **ones**. When you see ten units stacked together, they represent **10**. You count these by **tens**.

ONE   TEN

When you count base ten blocks, you always start with the larger amount first. For example, to count this set, you point to the **ten** first and say "ten." Then point to the ones blocks and keep counting up by **ones**: "eleven, twelve, thirteen."

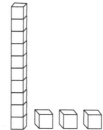

➡ COUNT each set of base ten blocks. CIRCLE the correct number.

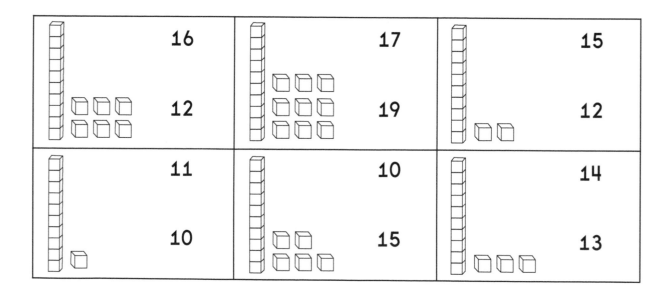

16	17	15
12	19	12
11	10	14
10	15	13

14. Thumbs Up or Down

Each place in a number is given a value that can be shown with **base ten blocks**. One base ten block represents **1**. You count these by **ones**. When you see ten units stacked together, they represent **10**. You count these by **tens**.

ONE ☐   TEN

When you count base ten blocks, you always start with the larger amount, or the **ten**, first.

➡ COUNT each set of base ten blocks. If the number above it is correct, COLOR in the thumbs up. If the number is incorrect, COLOR in the thumbs down.

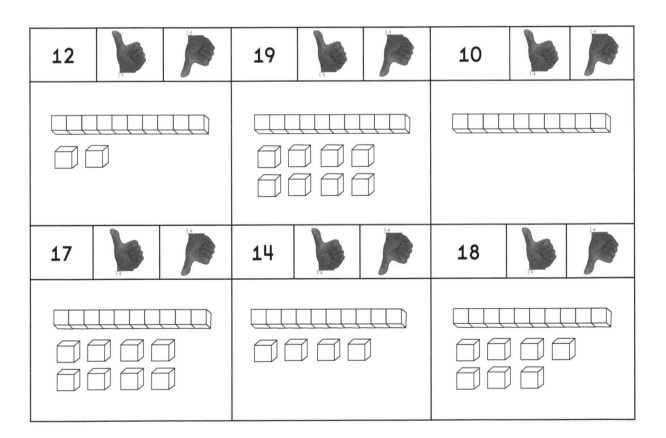

15. Billy's Blocks

Each place in a number is given a value that can be shown with **base ten blocks**. One base ten block represents **1**. You count these by **ones**. When you see ten units stacked together, they represent **10**. You count these by **tens**.

When you count base ten blocks, you always start with the larger amount, or the **ten**, first.

➡ LOOK at each number. COLOR the correct amount of base ten blocks needed to make that number.

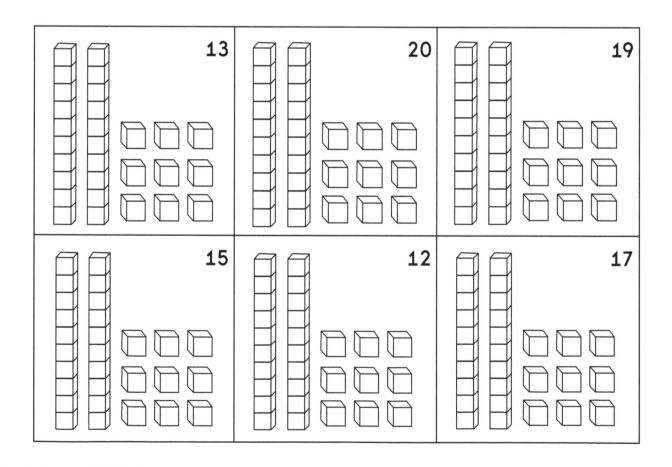

16. Keep on Counting

Each place in a number is given a value that can be shown with **base ten blocks**. One base ten block represents **1**. You count these by **ones**. When you see ten units stacked together, they represent **10**. You count these by **tens**.

ONE   TEN

When you count base ten blocks, you always start with the larger amount, or the **ten**, first.

➡ COUNT each set of base ten blocks. WRITE the correct number in the box.

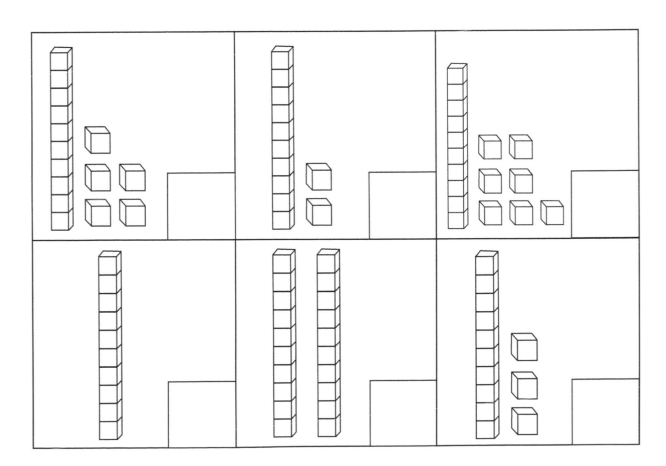

17. Adding Apples

Addition is when two numbers or groups are added together to find a total. A **total** is also called a **sum**. You can use pictures, your fingers, a number line, or objects to add numbers together!

An **equation** is a math problem written out with numbers and symbols.

Two numbers represent the groups being added together. The **+** symbol means add. The **=** symbol comes just before the number that tells the total after adding together.

➡ COUNT the first set of apples in each row. Continue counting the second set to find how many there are all together. WRITE the answer in the box.

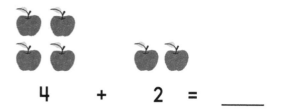

4   +   2   =   ____

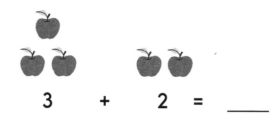

3   +   2   =   ____

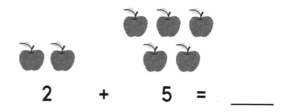

2   +   5   =   ____

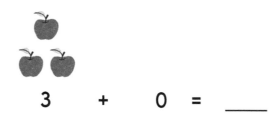

3   +   0   =   ____

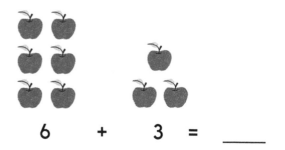

6   +   3   =   ____

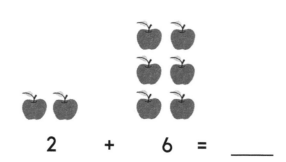

2   +   6   =   ____

Skill: Addition

18. Gift Tag Totals

Addition is when two numbers or groups are added together to find a total. A **total** is also called a **sum**. You can use pictures, your fingers, a number line, or objects to add numbers together!

An **equation** is a math problem written out with numbers and symbols.

These two numbers represent the groups being added together.

The **+** symbol means add, and the **=** symbol comes just before the number that tells the total after adding together.

$$1 + 2 = 3$$ —— **3** is the total.

➡ ADD the numbers together. WRITE the answer on the gift tag. COLOR the gift tag using the color in the key that matches the answer.

| 1 | 2 | 3 | 4 | 5 |

2 + 2 =	3 + 2 =
2 + 1 =	0 + 2 =
4 + 1 =	1 + 1 =
2 + 3 =	1 + 0 =

Skill: Addition

19. Addition Stories

Word problems are stories that can help **solve**, or find the answer to, a math problem. When reading the word problems, listen carefully to the numbers. ➡ READ the story first. FILL IN the numbers in the equation and use the blank space to DRAW a picture to match the story. You can use simple shapes to represent objects. SOLVE the addition problem and WRITE the correct answer.

1. Kayla had 3 pieces of candy. Her mom gave her 3 more. How many pieces does Kayla have now?

_____ + _____ = _____

2. Beau had 1 fish in his tank. He got 1 more from the pet store. How many fish does he have now?

_____ + _____ = _____

3. Renee had 5 crackers. She got 2 more out of the box. How many does she have now?

_____ + _____ = _____

4. Whit had 4 balls. His dad gave him 1 more ball. How many does he have now?

_____ + _____ = _____

Skill: Addition Word Problems

20. Follow the Rainbow

An **equation** is a math problem written out with numbers and symbols. There are many ways to add numbers together to make the number **10**. A rainbow is a fun way to see how the numbers work together to make **10**.
➡ LOOK at the equation. FIND the first number in the equation on the rainbow. FOLLOW that color to the other side to find the other number that gets added to make **10** and WRITE it in the blank.

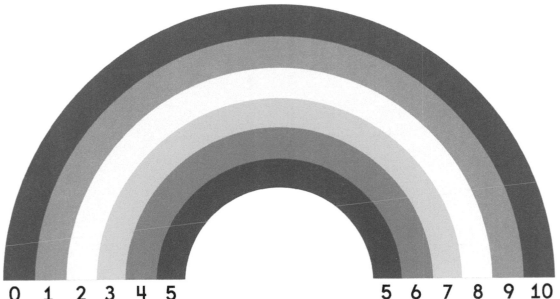

0   1   2   3   4   5   5   6   7   8   9   10

0 + _____ = 10   10 + _____ = 10

1 + _____ = 10   9 + _____ = 10

2 + _____ = 10   8 + _____ = 10

3 + _____ = 10   7 + _____ = 10

4 + _____ = 10   6 + _____ = 10

5 + _____ = 10   5 + _____ = 10

Skill: Making 10

21. Tens Frame Circles

There are many ways to add numbers together to make the number **10**. A **tens frame** is an easy way to see different ways to make **10**.

➡ LOOK at the tens frame. COUNT how many circles are already there. FIND that number in the equation. COLOR new circles with a different color to make ten total circles in the frame. Complete the equation. The first one is done for you as an example.

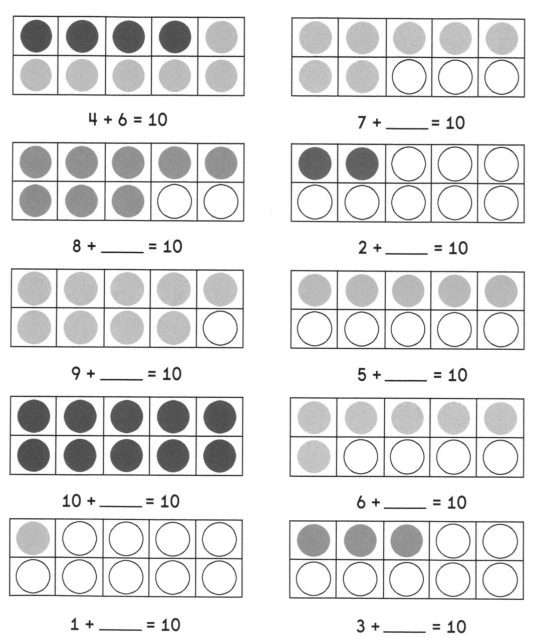

4 + 6 = 10

7 + _____ = 10

8 + _____ = 10

2 + _____ = 10

9 + _____ = 10

5 + _____ = 10

10 + _____ = 10

6 + _____ = 10

1 + _____ = 10

3 + _____ = 10

Skill: Making 10

22. Pet Patrol

There are many ways to add numbers together to make the same number. For example, 1+3=4, but also 2+2=4.

➡ DRAW a line to match the pet animals that are being added together to the correct number. You will draw a line to each number twice!

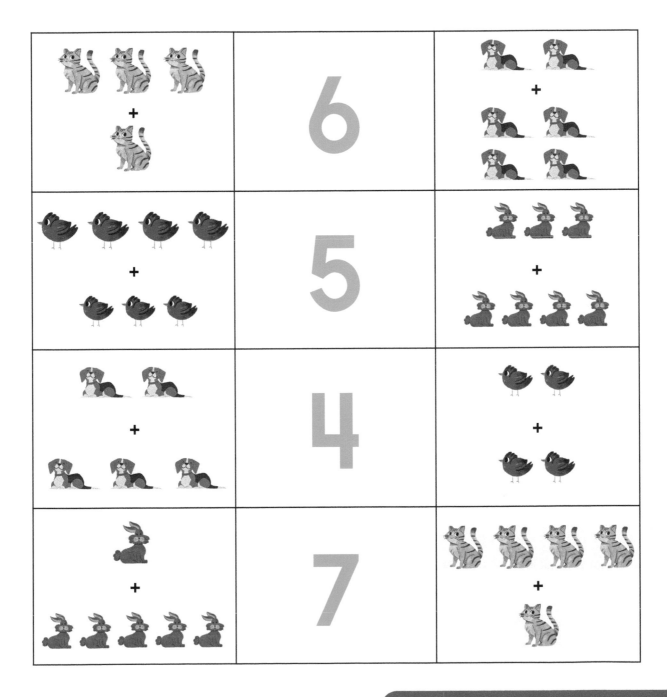

23. Falling Petals

Subtraction is when a group of objects or a number has some taken away. It's used to find how many are left. An **equation** is a math problem written out with numbers and symbols.

➡ LOOK at each equation. The first number shows how many objects are in the box. The second number shows how many to take away. CROSS OUT the objects to take them away. WRITE how many are left in the blank.

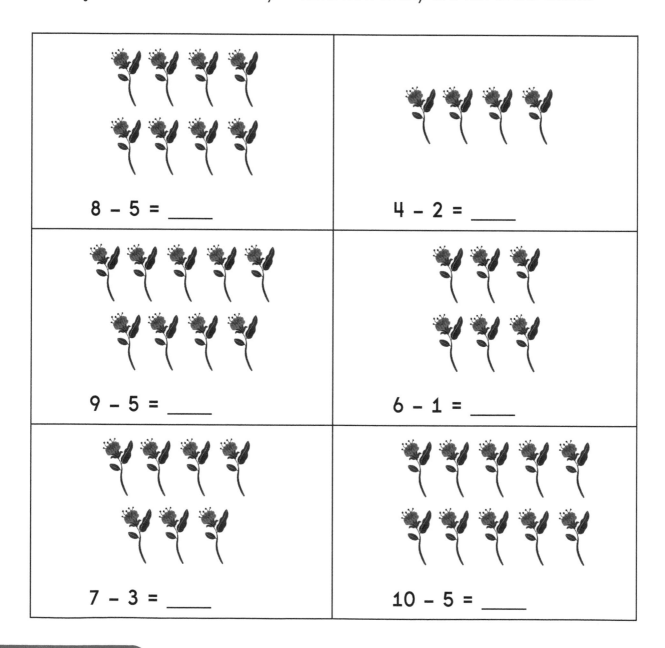

8 – 5 = _____

4 – 2 = _____

9 – 5 = _____

6 – 1 = _____

7 – 3 = _____

10 – 5 = _____

Skill: Subtraction

24. Subtraction Stories

Word problems are stories that can help to solve, or find the answer to, a subtraction problem. When reading the word problems, listen carefully to the numbers.

➥ FILL IN the numbers in the equation. Use the blank space to DRAW a picture to match the story. You can use simple shapes to represent objects. SOLVE the subtraction problem and WRITE the correct answer.

1. Heidi had 8 pieces of pop-corn. She ate 5 pieces. How many pieces does she have left? ____ - ____ = ____	**2.** Juan found 6 shells at the beach. He lost 4 shells in the water. How many does he have left? ____ - ____ = ____
3. Kennedy has 4 soccer balls. She gave 2 away to her friends. How many does she have left? ____ - ____ = ____	**4.** Hiro bought 2 baseball cards at the store. He gave 1 to his best friend. How many does he have left? ____ - ____ = ____

Skill: Subtraction Word Problems

25. School Supplies

Addition is when numbers get added together. Subtraction is when numbers are taken away. When reading equations, it is important to pay attention to the symbols.

➡ READ each equation. Use the pictures to SOLVE the problem and WRITE the answer. Remember to CROSS OUT pictures to help you solve the subtraction problems. Pay attention to the symbols!

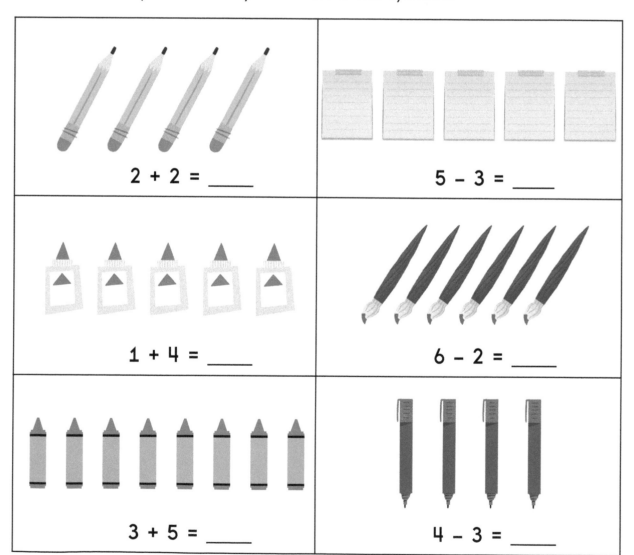

2 + 2 = ____

5 − 3 = ____

1 + 4 = ____

6 − 2 = ____

3 + 5 = ____

4 − 3 = ____

Skill: Addition and Subtraction

26. Fish Friends

Addition is when numbers get added together. Subtraction is when numbers are taken away. When reading equations, it is important to pay attention to the symbols.

➡ SOLVE the equation on each fish. WRITE the answer in the bubble. COLOR the fish with the color that matches the answer in the key.

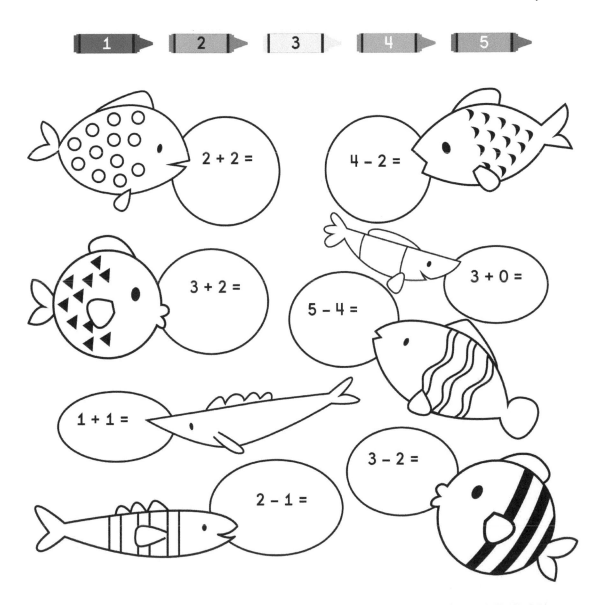

Skill: Addition and Subtraction

27. Short and Long

Length is used to measure how long something is. Words such as **shorter** and **longer** help compare two objects by length.

➡ LOOK at each set of objects. COLOR the shorter object blue. COLOR the longer object green.

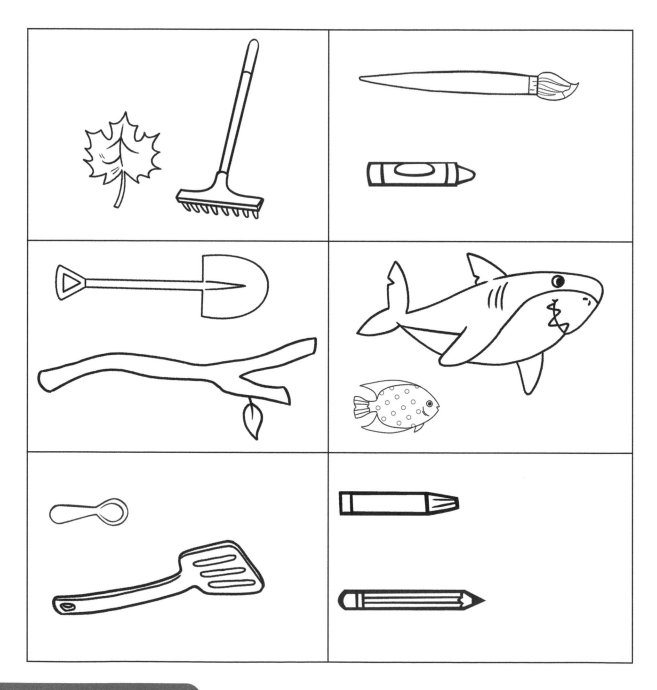

Skill: Comparing Length

28. Lighten Up

Weight is used to measure how heavy or light something is.
Words such as **lighter** and **heavier** are used to compare two objects
by weight.

   The feather is lighter than the elephant. The elephant
is heavier than the feather.

➥ LOOK at each object. DRAW an object beside it that would be lighter.

Skill: Comparing Weight

29. Short and Tall

Height is used to measure how short or tall something is. Words such as **shorter** and **taller** are used to compare two objects by height.

The boy is shorter than the girl. The girl is taller than the boy.

➡ LOOK at each object. CIRCLE the object that is taller. DRAW an **X** on the object that is shorter.

30. More or Less

Capacity is used to measure how much something can hold. Phrases such as **holds less** and **holds more** are used to compare two objects by capacity.
➡ LOOK at each object on the left. COMPARE it to the object on the right. FILL IN the blank with the words **more** or **less.**

The cup holds _____ than the bucket.

The pool holds _____ than the jug.

The kettle holds _____ than the bathtub.

The water bottle holds _____ than the pot.

The bowl holds _____ than the spoon.

The jar holds _____ than the vase.

Skill: Comparing Capacity

31. Shipshape

Size is uses to measure how big or small something is. Words such as **small**, **medium**, and **large** are used to compare objects by size.

SMALL   MEDIUM   LARGE

➡ LOOK at each set of shapes. CIRCLE the smallest shape. DRAW an **X** on the largest shape.

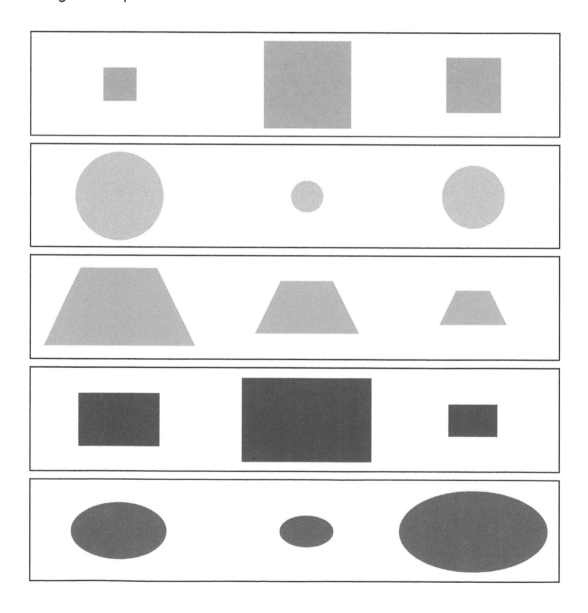

Skill: Comparing Size

32. Inch by Inch

Units are used to measure something. A ruler's **unit of measurement** is an inch.

➡ LOOK at the rulers below each pencil. Where the pencil's tip ends on the ruler, that is how many inches long the pencil is. MEASURE each pencil and WRITE the number in the box.

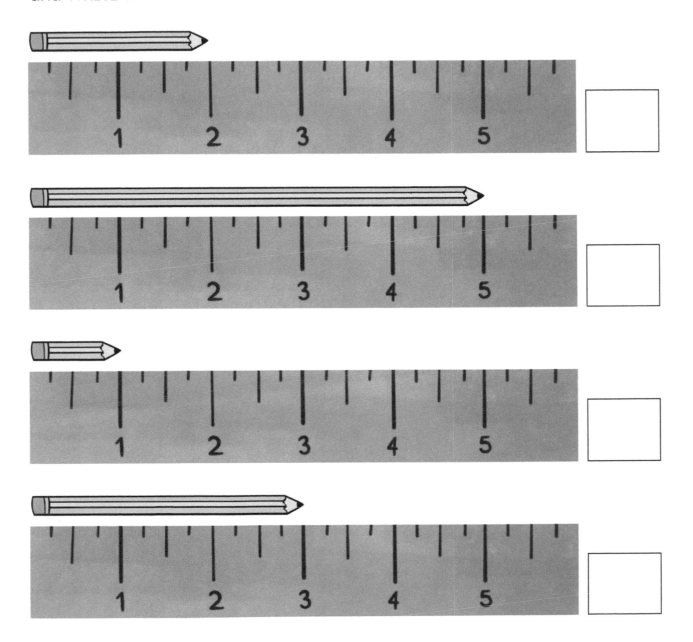

33. Reach for the Sky

Units are used to measure something. You can use lots of things as a **unit of measure**. In this activity, blocks are the units to measure how tall the flowers are.

➡ Each flower is a different height. Use the blocks beside the flower to COUNT how tall they are. WRITE the answer in the box.

| 5 |
| 4 |
| 3 |
| 2 |
| 1 |

| 5 |
| 4 |
| 3 |
| 2 |
| 1 |

| 5 |
| 4 |
| 3 |
| 2 |
| 1 |

| 5 |
| 4 |
| 3 |
| 2 |
| 1 |

Skill: Measuring Height

34. Flat Shapes

Shapes are everywhere! Everything is made of different shapes. 2D shapes are flat, like a piece of unfolded paper. POINT to each shape and SAY its name.

circle   triangle   square   rectangle   hexagon   rhombus

➡ COLOR each shape using the color that matches the shape on the key.

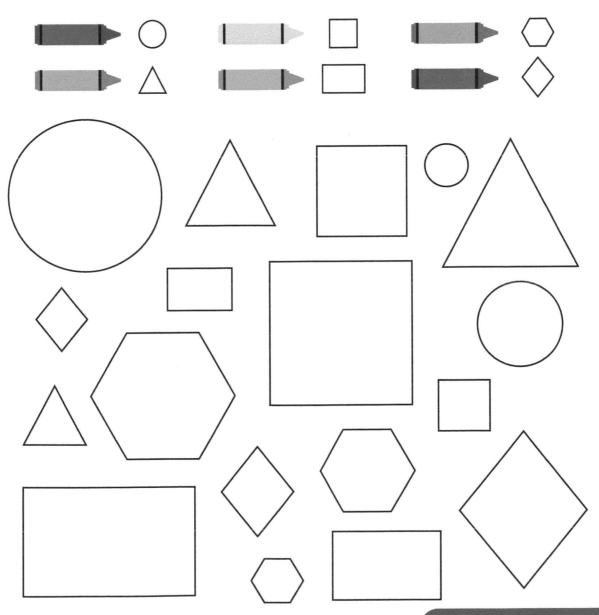

35. Shape Train

Shapes make up the world around us.
➡ LOOK at the train. WRITE how many of each shape you see on the train.

⬭○ ———— ☐ ———— ⬡ ————

△ ———— ▭ ———— ◇ ————

36. Do You See It?

Every object you see has a shape.

➡ LOOK at each object on the left that you might see in real life. DRAW a line to the matching shape.

37. Corners and Sides

Shapes have **corners** and **sides**. Corners are where the sides come together to a point.

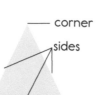
— corner
sides

➡ CIRCLE the corners on each shape. WRITE the number. COUNT how many sides each shape has. WRITE the number.

SHAPES	CORNERS	SIDES
○		
△		
□		
▭		
⬡		
◇		

Skill: Analyzing 2D Shapes

38. The Shape of Things

Shapes are everywhere! Everything is made of different shapes. 3D shapes are not flat like 2D shapes. 3D shapes are three-dimensional and take up more space. That means you can hold them in your hand or feel their many faces.

➡ POINT to each shape and say its name. COLOR each shape by using the color that matches the shape on the key.

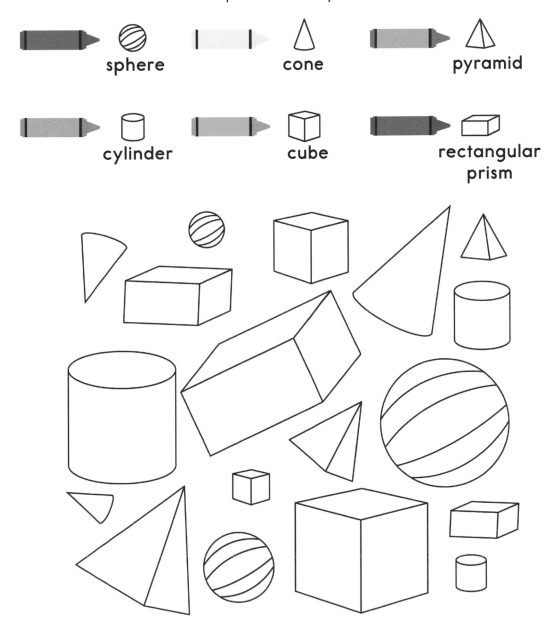

sphere   cone   pyramid

cylinder   cube   rectangular prism

Skill: Naming 3D Shapes

39. Shape Castle

Shapes make up the world around us.

➡ LOOK at the castle. WRITE how many of each shape you see on the castle.

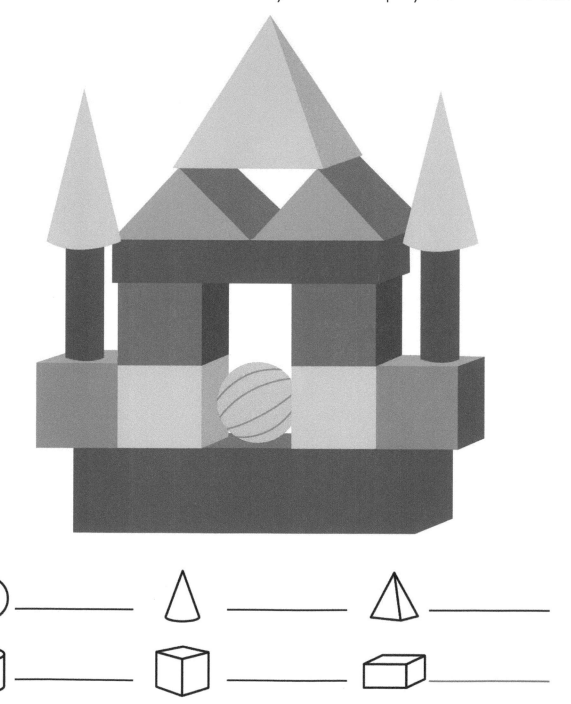

40. I See in 3D

Every object you see has a shape.

➡ LOOK at each object on the left that you might see in real life. DRAW a line to the matching shape.

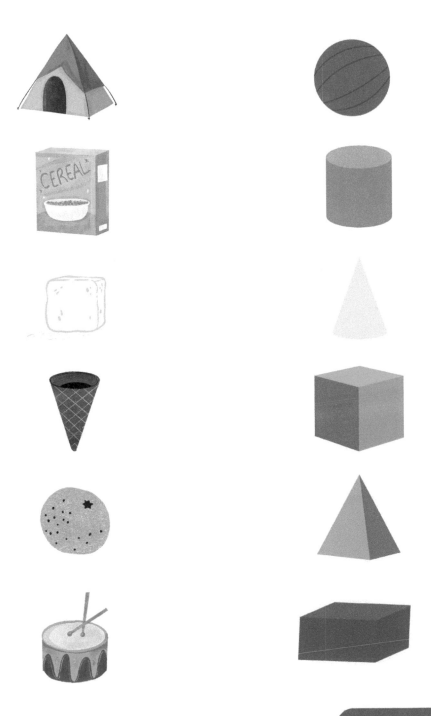

41. 2D vs. 3D

2D shapes are flat. 3D shapes are solid with many faces.
➡ LOOK at each shape. COLOR the shape using the color that matches the type of shape in the key.

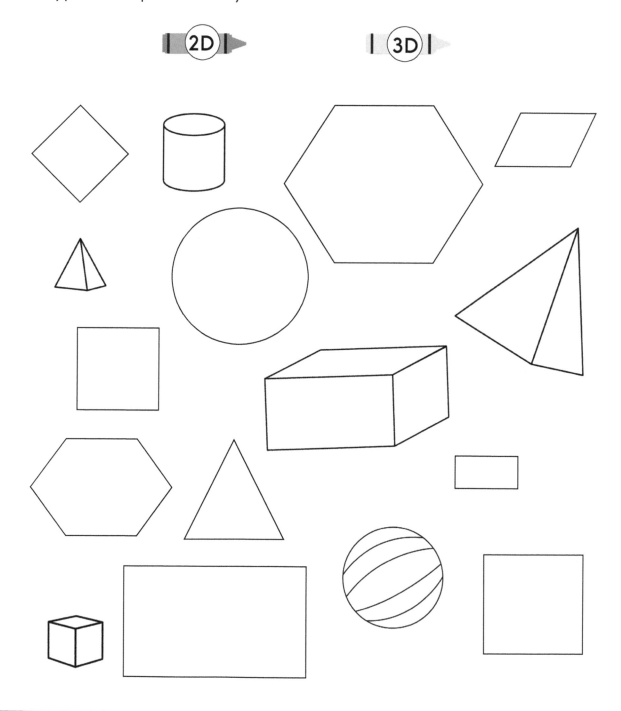

42. A New Dimension

2D shapes are flat. 3D shapes are solid with many faces.

➡ LOOK at each shape. CIRCLE whether the shape is 2D or 3D.

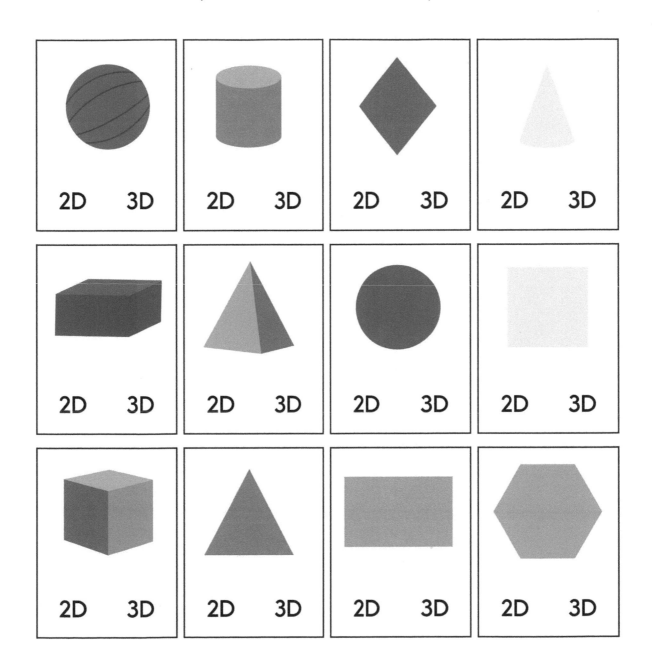

2D 3D	2D 3D
2D 3D	2D 3D

Skill: Analyzing 3D Shapes

43. A Lot Alike

2D and 3D shapes are different, but they have similar faces.
➡ LOOK at each 2D shape on the left. DRAW a line to the 3D shape that looks similar.

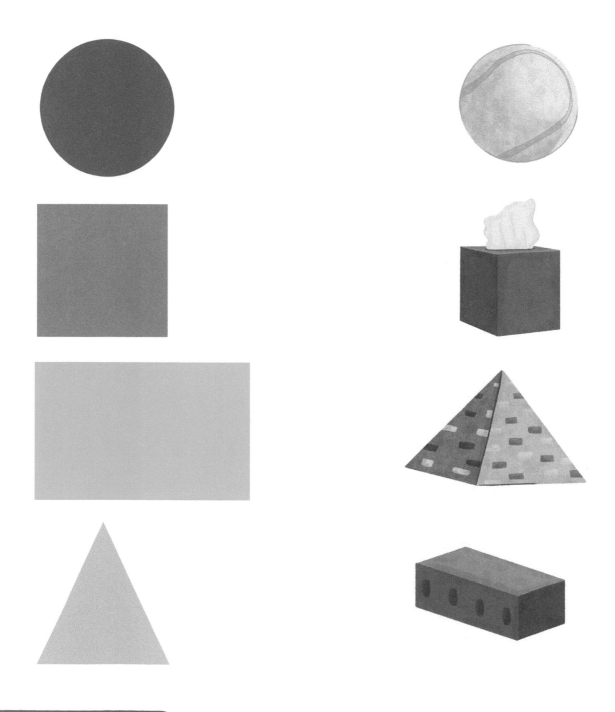

Skill: Analyzing Shapes

44. Shape Builder

Putting 2D shapes together can make new shapes!
➠ LOOK at the sets of shapes on the left. DRAW a line to the new shape they can make!

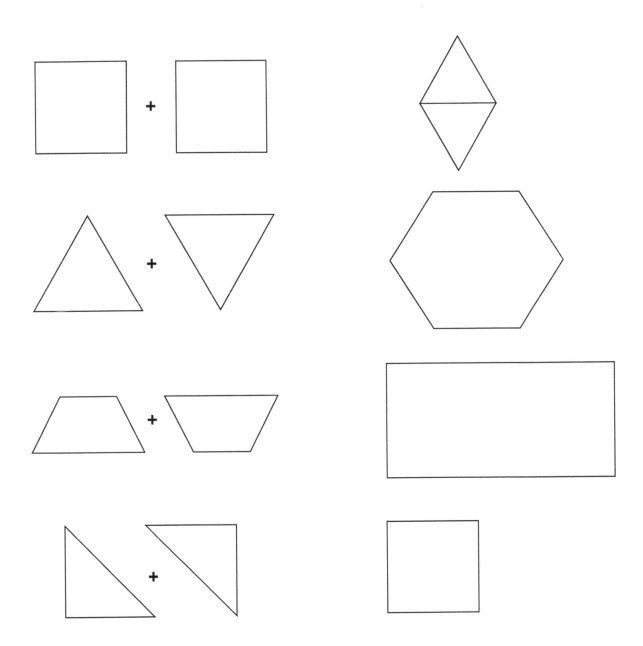

45. Hidden Shapes

Putting 2D shapes together can make new shapes!

➡ LOOK at the shapes. FIND the triangles hiding in the shapes and color them purple. FIND the squares and color them blue.

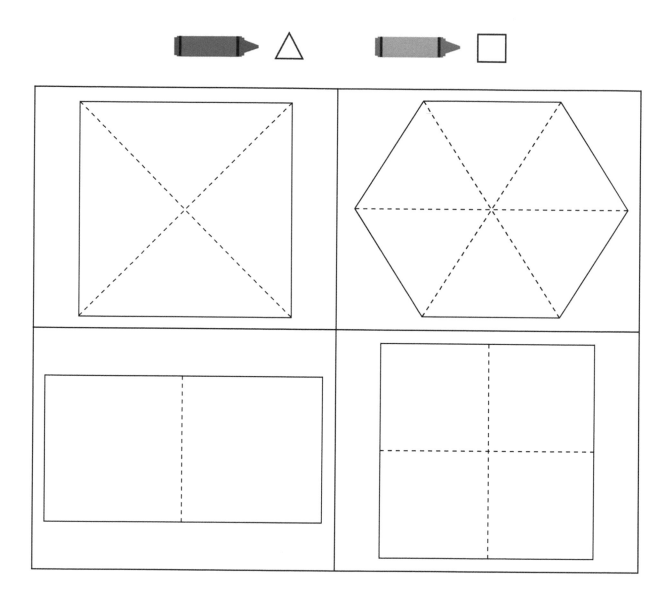

Certificate of Completion

This certificate is presented to

_____

for learning skills to read, write, and do math!

▼▲▼▲▼▲▼▲▼▲▼▲▼▲▼▲▼▲▼▲▼▲▼▲▼▲▼▲▼

Date _____

Answer Key

Part 1: Reading

1. and 2. Alphabet Train

3. Match It Up!

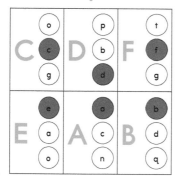

4. Bug Buddies

5. Color Match

L	N	O	M	N
N	M	P	L	P
O	L	O	N	M
M	P	P	O	L

6. Pair the Pair

R	a	(r)	c
Q	(q)	p	f
T	h	j	(t)
S	(s)	r	n
U	a	b	(u)

7. Plane Pals

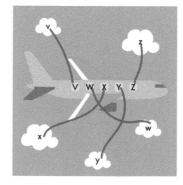

8. Letter or Word?

(s)	hat	(t)
bed	(W)	pig
(o)	(p)	rag

9. Word or Sentence?

the · **The grass is green.** · baby

I love you! · **Do you see it?** · see

This is fun! · play · **I can run.**

water · **I love school!** · ball

10. Smiley Spaces

I 🙂 am 🙂 five 🙂 years🙂 old.

My 🙂 dog🙂 is 🙂 black.

Did 🙂 you 🙂 see 🙂 the 🙂 book?

Do 🙂 you 🙂 like 🙂 ice 🙂 cream?

I 🙂 love 🙂 jumping!

We 🙂 like 🙂 to 🙂 yell!

11. What's That Sound?

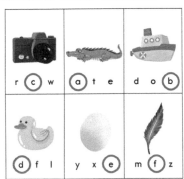

r (c) w | (a) t e | d o (b)

(d) f l | y x (e) | m (f) z

12. Match the Letter

G H I J K

13. This or That

X(n) | X(p) | (l)X

(o)X | X(m) | (q)X

14. Bubble Letters

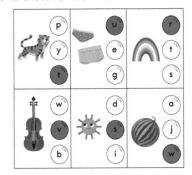

p / y / t | u / e / g | r / t / s

w / v / b | d / s / i | a / j / w

15. Sound Finder

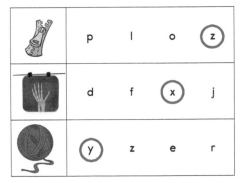

	p	l	o	(z)
	d	f	(x)	j
	(y)	z	e	r

16. Rhyme Time

17. Connect the Rhyme

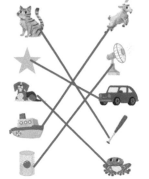

18. Clap to the Beat

1 **②**	**①** 2	1 **②**
① 2	**①** 2	1 **②**

19. Clap, Count, and Color

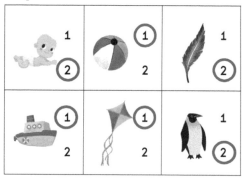

20. Sound Off!

(bed) | led   run | (sun)   (rat) | bat

dad | (sad)   bug | (rug)   (pig) | dig

21. What's the Word?

net
bug
bag
fox
fan
bus
pot
cup

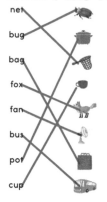

22. Middle Match

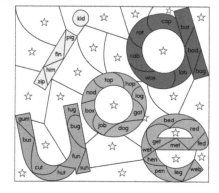

(hat) | hit   sax | (six)   (cut) | cat

mud | (mad) (log) | leg   pan | (pen)

23. Vowel Hunt

24. Which Vowel?

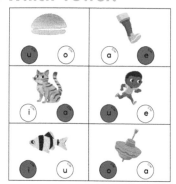

u o	a e
i a	u e
i u	o a

25. The Perfect Ending

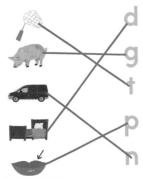

d

g

t

p

n

26. Sounds the Same

27. Find the Word

tub	bib	dad
fed	pin	jam

28. Meet the "at" Family

h at

c at

m at

r at

b at

29. Visit the "ed" Family

bed	bed		
red	red		
fed	fed		
wed	wed		
Ted	Ted		

30. The "ig" Family Lives Here

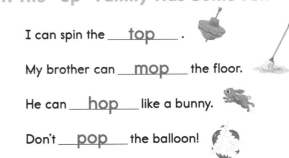

31. The "op" Family Has Some Fun

I can spin the ___top___ .

My brother can ___mop___ the floor.

He can ___hop___ like a bunny.

Don't ___pop___ the balloon!

32. Color the "ug" Family

hug	tug	bug	dug
hat	fig	jug	wed
mug	pot	pan	rig
fed	pug	cat	rug

33. The Long and Short of It

34. The Great Silent E

kite

robe

cane

tape

cape

35. Silent E Goes to Work

The dog has a __bone__ .

A clock tells us the __time__ .

I like to ride my __bike__ .

My family lives in a __home__ .

Bees make honey in a __hive__ .

36. The Playful Pig

Who likes to play in the mud?

(pig)   dog

Where does he play in the mud?

in the house   (at the farm)

What does he need after playing in the mud?

(a bath)   a cookie

37. A Dog's Bone

What is the dog's name?

__Spot__

What did the child give the dog?

__bone__

Where did the dog bury it?

__backyard__

38. Beach Day

Answers may vary

39. The Cat on the Mat

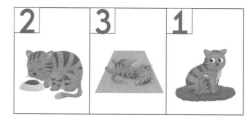

40. Words You Don't Know

My dad puts me on his __shoulders__ .

We like to build __sandcastles__ at the beach.

Flowers need sunlight, soil, and __water__ to live.

Penguins are a type of __bird__ .

I use a rake to gather __leaves__ .

41. Jim's Rocks

What do you think the word collect means?

☐ (gather)   ☐ eat

What do you think the word discover means?

☐ cook   ☐ find

What do you think the word lusters means?

☐ (shininess)   ☐ faces

42. Picture Clues

	☑ a sleepy cat
	☐ a hungry monkey
	☐ a train ride
	☑ a rainy day
	☐ a slumber party
	☑ a day at the zoo
	☑ a baseball game
	☐ a day at school

43. All about Sharks

Sharks live in the ocean. Sharks have many teeth that they lose and replace often. Sharks cannot see color. Most sharks live for about 25 years. Have you ever seen a shark?

44. A Couple of Caterpillars

What are both of these stories about?

☑ caterpillars ☐ monkeys

What is one thing that they both like to do?

☐ basketball ☑ fishing

How are Cam and Cassie different?

<u>   Answers will vary   </u>

45. Parts of a Book

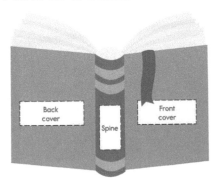

Back cover

Spine

Front cover

Part 2: Writing

1. ABC Practice

A A A A A A A

a a a a a a a a

B B B B B B B

b b b b b b b

C C C C C C

c c c c c c c c

2. D Is for Dog

D D D D D D

d d d d d d

E E E E E E

e e e e e e e

F F F F F F F

f f f f f f f

3. G Is for Gorilla

G G G G G

g g g g g g g

H H H H H H H

h h h h h h h h

I I I I I I I I I I I

i i i i i i i i i i i i i i

4. J Is for Jellyfish

J J J J J J J

j j j j j j j j j

K K K K K K

k k k k k k k

L L L L L L L

l l l l l l l l l l l

5. M Is for Monkey

M M M M M

m m m m m m m

N N N N N

n n n n n n n

O O O O O

o o o o o o o o o

6. P Is for Pig

P P P P P P P

p p p p p p p

Q Q Q Q Q

q q q q q q q

R R R R R R R

r r r r r r r r r r

7. S Is for Snake

S S S S S S S S

s s s s s s s s s s

T T T T T T T T

t t t t t t t t t t t

U U U U U U U

u u u u u u u u

8. V Is for Volcano

V V V V V V

v v v v v v v v

W W W W W

w w w w w w w w

X X X X X X

x x x x x x x x x

9. Z Is for Zebra

Y Y Y Y Y Y

y y y y y y y y

Z Z Z Z Z

z z z z z z z z z

10. All the Uppercase Letters

A	B	C	D
E	F	G	H
I	J	K	L
M	N	O	P
Q	R	S	T
U	V	W	X
Y	Z		

11. All the Lowercase Letters

a	b	c	d
e	f	g	h
i	j	k	l
m	n	o	p
q	r	s	t
u	v	w	x
y	z		

12. Flower Power

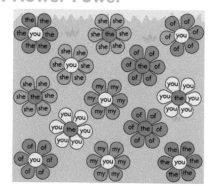

13. Sight Word Hide-and-Seek

14. Crossword Critters

15. See It and Say It

1. I love to ___eat___ apples.

2. I will ___get___ a book off the shelf.

3. We like pizza ___with___ pepperoni on top.

4. This cookie is ___good___ .

5. I look ___like___ my dad.

15. See It and Say It

17. Draw Your Own

Answers may vary

18. Plural Pictures

19. Game, Set, Match!

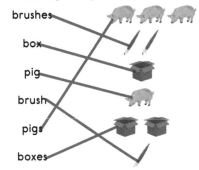

brushes

box

pig

brush

pigs

boxes

20. Verbs in Action

21. What Are They Doing?

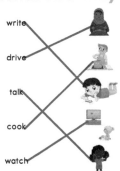

write

drive

talk

cook

watch

22. Verb and Noun Showdown

eat	cry	dog
noun | (verb)	noun | (verb)	(noun) | verb
sleep	swim	rabbit
noun | (verb)	noun | (verb)	(noun) | verb

23. All About Firefighters

24. Question Time!

1. **Where** should we go to see the animals?
2. **How** did this nest get in the tree?
3. **Who** helps us feel better?
4. **What** food do I need to buy from the store?
5. **When** will we have your graduation party?
6. **Why** do squirrels gather nuts?

25. Where, Oh, Where?

(BEHIND) | BELOW	IN | (ON)	(BELOW) | BETWEEN
(BETWEEN) | BEHIND	(IN) | ON	BEHIND | (BY)

26. The Great Outdoors

27. Where Did It Go?

The bear is __in__ the wagon.	The boy is __below__ the kite.
The girl is __behind__ the chair.	The monkey is __between__ the trees.
The table is __by__ the couch.	The cat is __on__ the rug.

28. A Capital Start

birds can fly.
Birds can fly.

koalas can climb.
Koalas can climb.

monkeys like bananas.
Monkeys like bananas.

fish have gills.
Fish have gills.

birds eat bugs.
Birds eat bugs.

29. Pick the Punctuation

	.	!	?
No way	☐	■	☐
My bike is green	■	☐	☐
What is your name	☐	☐	■
Her ball is big	■	☐	☐
Look at me	☐	■	☐
How old are you	☐	☐	■

30. Let's Go See the Animals!

An octopus has eight legs.

That elephant is huge!

Pigs like to roll in mud.

How do fish move?

There's a snake!

What do rabbits eat?

31. Match Madness

I see a big bed.

I like to dig.

I see a fan.

The dog can sit.

The cat is orange.

My rug is red.

32. Your Choice

Answers may vary.

33. At the Park

Answers may vary.

34. All About Me

Answers may vary.

35. Animal Fact Finder

Answers may vary.

36. That's a Fact

Fish have scales.		FACT	OPINION
Insects are cool.		FACT	OPINION
A lion's baby is a cub.		FACT	OPINION
An eagle is a type of bird.		FACT	OPINION
Baby elephants are so cute.		FACT	OPINION
A rabbit is a fun pet.		FACT	OPINION

37. The Fact of the Matter

ICE CREAM		Ice cream is cold.
		Ice cream is the best dessert.
TURTLE		Turtles have shells.
		Turtles are cool animals.
IGLOO		I would love to live in an igloo.
		Igloos are made of ice.
HORSE		Horses can gallop.
		I like to ride horses.
BOAT		Boats are fun to watch.
		Boats can float on water.
FROG		Frogs lay eggs.
		Frogs are neat.

38. How to Brush Your Teeth

Answers may vary.

39. How to Clean Your Room

Answers may vary.

40. Think About It

Answers may vary.

41. Show-and-Tell

Answers may vary.

42. Jen's Snow Day

Answers may vary.

43. Pat's Cat

first	second	third

First, Pat got a new ___cat___.

Next, Pat gave his cat ___food___.

Last, Pat played with his cat with a ___toy___.

44. Ren Goes to School

45. Mei Plants a Flower

Part 3: Math

1. Numbers Are Everywhere

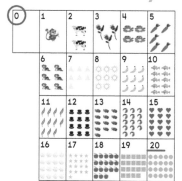

2. Number Bugs

3. Fruit Salad

4. Count the Raindrops

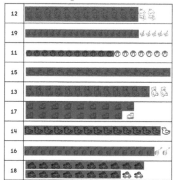

5. In the Toy Box

12
19
11
15
13
17
14
16
18

6. Fun in the Sun

	6
	12
	18
	8
	10
	2
	14
	19

7. A Trip to the Candy Shop

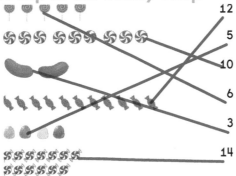

8. Summer Reading Challenge

Who read the most books?
__Kevin__

Who read fewer books than Aisha?
__Nate__

Who read the least books?
__Nate__

Which two kids read an equal number of books?
__Aisha and Wendy__

Who read more books than Jamal? __Kevin__

9. Hot Rod Numbers

10. Up to 100!

1	2	3	4	5	6	7	8	9	10
11	12	13	14	15	16	17	18	19	20
21	22	23	24	25	26	27	28	29	30
31	32	33	34	35	36	37	38	39	40
41	42	43	44	45	46	47	48	49	50
51	52	53	54	55	56	57	58	59	60
61	62	63	64	65	66	67	68	69	70
71	72	73	74	75	76	77	78	79	80
81	82	83	84	85	86	87	88	89	90
91	92	93	94	95	96	97	98	99	100

11. The Case of the Missing Numbers

1	2	3	4	5	6	7	8	9	10
11	12	13	14	15	16	17	18	19	20
21	22	23	24	25	26	27	28	29	30
31	32	33	34	35	36	37	38	39	40
41	42	43	44	45	46	47	48	49	50
51	52	53	54	55	56	57	58	59	60
61	62	63	64	65	66	67	68	69	70
71	72	73	74	75	76	77	78	79	80
81	82	83	84	85	86	87	88	89	90
91	92	93	94	95	96	97	98	99	100

12. Sunshine Sequence

12 - 13 - 14 - 15 - 16

45 - 46 - 47 - 48 - 49

3 - 4 - 5 - 6 - 7

86 - 87 - 88 - 89 - 90

22 - 23 - 24 - 25 - 26

13. Count the Blocks

16, 17, 15
12, 19, 12
11, 10, 14
10, 15, 13

14. Thumbs Up or Down

12, 19, 10
17, 14, 18

15. Billy's Blocks

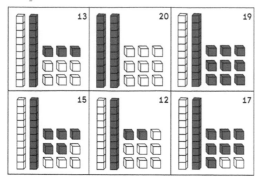

16. Keep on Counting

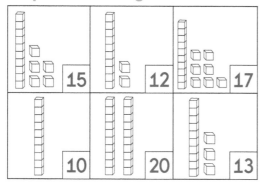

17. Adding Apples

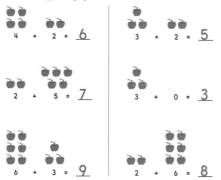

4 + 2 = 6   3 + 2 = 5

2 + 5 = 7   3 + 0 = 3

6 + 3 = 9   2 + 6 = 8

18. Gift Tag Totals

2 + 2 = 4	3 + 2 = 5
2 + 1 = 3	0 + 2 = 2
4 + 1 = 5	1 + 1 = 2
2 + 3 = 5	1 + 0 = 1

19. Addition Stories

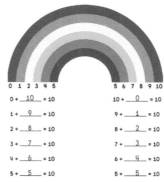

1. Kayla had 3 pieces of candy. Her mom gave her 3 more. How many pieces does Kayla have now?

2. Beau had 1 fish in his tank. He got 1 more from the pet store. How many fish does he have now?

Pictures will vary.

3 + 3 = 6   1 + 1 = 2

3. Renee had 5 crackers. She got 2 more out of the box. How many does she have now?

4. Whit had 4 balls. His dad gave him 1 more ball. How many does he have now?

Pictures will vary.

5 + 2 = 7   4 + 1 = 5

20. Follow the Rainbow

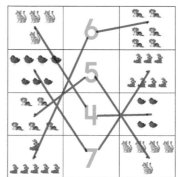

0 1 2 3 4 5   5 6 7 8 9 10

0 + 10 = 10   10 + 0 = 10

1 + 9 = 10   9 + 1 = 10

2 + 8 = 10   8 + 2 = 10

3 + 7 = 10   7 + 3 = 10

4 + 6 = 10   6 + 4 = 10

5 + 5 = 10   5 + 5 = 10

21. Tens Frame Circles

4 + 6 = 10   7 + 3 = 10

8 + 2 = 10   2 + 8 = 10

9 + 1 = 10   5 + 5 = 10

10 + 0 = 10   6 + 4 = 10

1 + 9 = 10   3 + 7 = 10

22. Pet Patrol

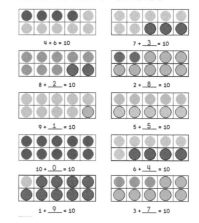

23. Falling Petals

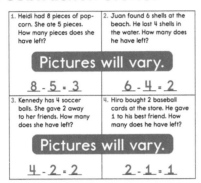

24. Subtraction Stories

1. Heidi had 8 pieces of popcorn. She ate 5 pieces. How many pieces does she have left?	2. Juan found 6 shells at the beach. He lost 4 shells in the water. How many does he have left?
Pictures will vary.	Pictures will vary.
$8 - 5 = 3$	$6 - 4 = 2$
3. Kennedy has 4 soccer balls. She gave 2 away to her friends. How many does she have left?	4. Hiro bought 2 baseball cards at the store. He gave 1 to his best friend. How many does he have left?
Pictures will vary.	Pictures will vary.
$4 - 2 = 2$	$2 - 1 = 1$

25. School Supplies

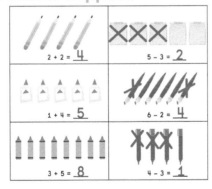

26. Fish Friends

27. Short and Long

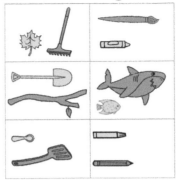

28. Lighten Up

Answers may vary.

29. Short and Tall

30. More or Less

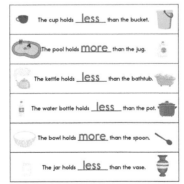

31. Shipshape

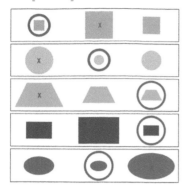

32. Inch by Inch

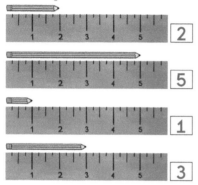

33. Reach for the Sky

34. Flat Shapes

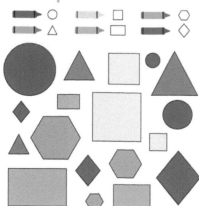

35. Shape Train

○ — 3   □ — 2   ⬡ — 3
△ — 2   ▭ — 3   ◇ — 6

36. Do You See It?

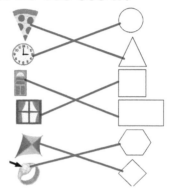

37. Corners and Sides

SHAPES	CORNERS	SIDES
○	0	0
△	3	3
◇	4	4
▭	4	4
⬡	6	6
◇	4	4

38. The Shape of Things

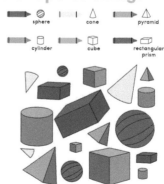

sphere   cone   pyramid
cylinder   cube   rectangular prism

39. Shape Castle

○ —1— △ —2— △ —3—
⊟ —2— ⬜ —6— ⬛ —2—

40. I See in 3D

41. 2D vs. 3D

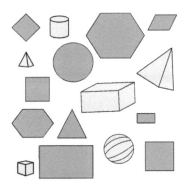

42. A New Dimension

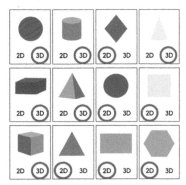

43. A Lot Alike

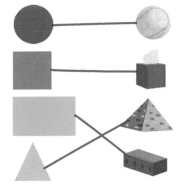

44. Shape Builder

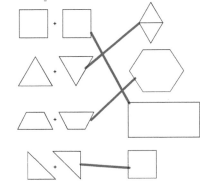

45. Hidden Shapes

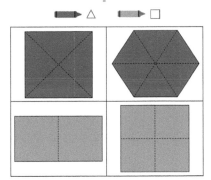

About the Author

Hayley Lewallen is the teacher and founder behind the Primary Post (ThePrimaryPost.com). She spent several years teaching kindergarten before deciding to stay home and teach her own small children. Through her website, Hayley loves creating resources and sharing fun ideas to make the lives of teachers and parents easier.